THE
WICKED WIT OF
QUEEN
ELIZABETH II

THE
WICKED WIT OF
QUEEN
ELIZABETH II

Compiled, edited
and introduced by

Karen Dolby

Michael O'Mara Books Limited

First published in Great Britain in 2015 by
Michael O'Mara Books Limited
9 Lion Yard
Tremadoc Road
London SW4 7NQ

A CIP catalogue record for this book is
available from the British Library.

Papers used by Michael O'Mara Books Limited are
natural, recyclable products made from wood grown in
sustainable forests. The manufacturing processes conform
to the environmental regulations of the country of origin.

ISBN: 978-1-78243-365-1 in hardback print format
ISBN: 978-1-78243-366-8 in e-book format

10

www.mombooks.com

Interior images © Alpha-Globe Photos, Inc/ImageCollect

Cover design by vaguelymemorable.com

Designed and typeset by Tetragon, London

Printed and bound
by CPI Group (UK) Ltd, Croydon, CRO 4YY

Contents

Introduction

When we think of the Queen our perception is one of dignity and authority. She is a serious figure: Her Majesty, the British monarch and head of the Commonwealth. But as anyone who has ever met her will tell you, in person she is very warm and human with a well-developed sense of humour. Look at it another way, could she have survived all these years doing what she does without being able to see the funny side of life?

The former Archbishop of Canterbury Dr Rowan Williams has said that the Queen can be 'extremely funny in private'. Having never had any contact with royalty before taking up his post, he had no idea what to expect. During numerous meetings he discovered someone with 'real personality': 'I have found in the Queen someone who can be friendly, who can be informal, who can be extremely funny in private – and not everybody appreciates how funny she can be.' He also realized she is 'quite prepared to tease and to be teased and who, while retaining her dignity always, doesn't stand on her dignity in a conversation'.

At her coronation on 2 June 1953 in Westminster Abbey, Queen Elizabeth II took the coronation oath vowing to serve her people and maintain the laws of God. What none of the 8,000 guests packed into the Abbey or the millions watching on television sets around the world heard was the Queen's frantic whisper to Archbishop Geoffrey Fisher to 'Get me started!' Friction between her heavy state robes and the carpet had her firmly fixed to the spot and she needed a firm push to get her going.

In a radio broadcast later that evening Elizabeth pledged, 'Throughout all my life and with all my heart I shall strive to be worthy of your trust.' For over sixty years she has done just that. And what a reign. Born in a time when one 'did one's duty', didn't spill the beans and emotions were kept in check, Elizabeth has seen society change beyond all recognition.

When she ascended the throne Britain was a drab place still in the grip of post-war austerity and rationing. The coronation gave a huge boost to sales of television sets – strictly black and white with only the BBC until 1955. Only 30 per cent of homes had washing machines, a mere 15 per cent owned a fridge and fewer still possessed a telephone. The world has changed rapidly since that time, for the Queen as much as for her subjects.

The swinging sixties, with their message of peace and love, gave way to the strikes and three-day week of the seventies, the shoulder-padded get-rich eighties, the poll tax riots of the nineties and the hope of a new millennium. Prime ministers have come and gone – the Queen has appointed and met with them all, coming close to the record set by her ancestor George III who saw off fourteen.

The royal family has faced ructions, rifts, scandals, divorces and deaths, including that of Princess Diana, when the fate of the monarchy itself seemed precarious. Following the emotional outpouring after Diana's death, the monarchy had to adapt. The past formality had to be relaxed and gradually the public has been allowed in to see the real person behind the crown. The Queen learned to show more of the warmth and cheeriness, the human side of her character that friends and family who were close to her had always known was there.

As Richard Crossman, the socialist politician and diarist, wrote after meeting the Queen in the 1960s, 'I noticed this time even more than last how shy she can be … She laughs with her whole face and she cannot just assume a mere smile because she's really a very spontaneous person … When she is deeply moved and tries to control it, she looks like an angry thundercloud. So very often when she has been deeply touched by the plaudits of the crowd she merely looks terribly bad-tempered.'

The Queen does not give interviews and those who know her best are trusted for a reason and simply don't talk. There is a suspicion that most of her best lines are said off-camera to her close inner circle. We catch glimpses and the odd unguarded remark. But watching her excitement at the races when one of her horses romps home to victory, or hearing how she danced a jig of delight at the news of an England test cricket victory, it's impossible to doubt she likes to have fun.

A certain twinkle in the royal eye, a flash of icy disapproval, the occasional cutting comment and quick quip all suggest a wicked wit. Like the rest of her family she's not above poking fun at herself and no one is safe from her love of a good joke. The Queen has been known to terrorize unsuspecting guests with her wild driving and is said to be a good mimic. When off-duty with her family she enjoys practical jokes and has a great sense of the absurd.

And besides, she's married to Prince Philip, at her side throughout all those banquets, royal performances, state occasions and visits. Someone who has chosen as her consort the gaffe-prone prince, whose comments have landed him in hot water on more than one occasion, cannot fail to have a well-developed sense of humour.

And her public love her for it. After scenes of adoring crowds lining the streets hoping for a glimpse of the Queen as her golden carriage rolled past at her Diamond Jubilee, or on the balcony after William and Kate's wedding, her position has never seemed more secure.

This book looks at the Queen's funny side through her own words as well as stories the rest of the family tell about her and the odd aside from Prince Philip. Occasionally unintentional, sometimes sarcastic and at other times downright silly, royal humour touches on every aspect of life. And over the years there has been ample opportunity for a right royal laugh.

Let us not take ourselves too seriously.
None of us has a monopoly on wisdom.

THE QUEEN
speaking in her Christmas broadcast, 1991

Timeline
of Queen Elizabeth II's Life

1926   Elizabeth Alexandra Mary was born at 2.40 a.m. on 21 April at 17 Bruton Street in Mayfair, London, to Elizabeth Bowes-Lyon, Duchess of York, and Prince Albert, Duke of York. She was christened on 29 May in the private chapel at Buckingham Palace.

1932   Her parents made the Royal Lodge in Windsor Great Park their country home. The family also lived at 145 Piccadilly in London and White Lodge in Richmond Park.

1936   The young Princess Elizabeth's life changed completely when her uncle King Edward VIII abdicated on 11 December to marry divorcee Wallis Simpson. Elizabeth's father became King George VI.

1940   On 13 October Princess Elizabeth delivered her first public broadcast on *Children's Hour* on BBC radio. Her younger sister, Margaret, joined her to say, 'Goodnight children,' at the end.

1942   Elizabeth was confirmed on 28 March in the private chapel at Windsor Castle.

1945   In February the princess joined the Women's Auxiliary Territorial Service as an honorary second subaltern; she trained as a driver and mechanic and was promoted to honorary junior commander a few months later.

1947   A big year. The princess went on her first overseas tour with her parents. On 9 July her engagement to Prince Philip of Greece and Denmark was announced. Philip then gave up his Greek and Danish titles and adopted his mother's British family surname, Mountbatten. He was created Duke of Edinburgh just before Elizabeth and Philip married on 20 November at Westminster Abbey.

1948   On 14 November Prince Charles was born. At the time the royal couple lived near Windsor Castle at Windlesham Moor, which they leased.

1949   Elizabeth, Philip and baby Charles moved to Clarence House in London on 4 July.

1950   Elizabeth and Margaret's beloved and trusted former governess Marion Crawford published *The Little Princesses*, a book of anecdotes about her life with the young princesses. This breach of trust was never forgotten or forgiven and any future betrayals were referred to as 'doing a Crawfie'.

Princess Anne, the Princess Royal, was born on 15 August.

1952   Elizabeth was proclaimed Queen on 6 February on the death of her father, King George VI. She heard the news while away on tour in Kenya.

1953   The coronation took place on 2 June in Westminster Abbey. On 24 November the Queen and Prince Philip began a six-month tour of the Commonwealth.

1954   In May the Queen and Prince Philip returned home on board the newly commissioned royal yacht *Britannia*, to a rapturous welcome from the British public.

1960   Prince Andrew was born on 19 February. Elizabeth was the first reigning monarch to give birth since Queen Victoria, whose youngest child, Princess Beatrice, was born in 1857.

Princess Margaret married Antony Armstrong-Jones (Lord Snowdon) on 6 May.

1964   Prince Edward was born on 10 March.

1969   Prince Charles's investiture as Prince of Wales took place at Caernarfon Castle on 1 July.

1970   The first ever royal walkabout took place during the Queen's visit to Australia and New Zealand with Prince Philip.

1977   Silver Jubilee celebrations marked twenty-five years on the throne. Princess Anne gave birth to Peter Phillips, the first of the Queen and Prince Philip's grandchildren, on 15 November.

1978   Princess Margaret and Lord Snowdon divorced.

1981   The engagement of Prince Charles and Lady Diana Spencer was announced on 24 February. Their wedding took place on 29 July in St Paul's Cathedral.

Princess Anne's second child, Zara Phillips, was born on 15 May.

The Queen was shot at during the Trooping of the Colour on 13 June. Seventeen-year-old Marcus Sarjeant fired six blanks and was quickly arrested. The Queen calmed her startled horse and carried on with the procession.

1982   Prince William was born on 21 June. He became second in line to the throne after his father Prince Charles.

The Queen's safety hit the headlines once more when Michael Fagan broke into Buckingham Palace and appeared in her bedroom in July.

1984   Princess Diana gave birth to Prince Harry on 15 September.

1986   Prince Andrew married Sarah Ferguson in July. They were made Duke and Duchess of York.

1988   Princess Beatrice was born on 8 August. As Prince Andrew's eldest child she is the Queen's sixth grandchild and sixth in line to the throne.

1990   The Duke and Duchess of York's youngest daughter, Princess Eugenie, was born on 23 March.

1992   The Queen's *annus horribilis*. In March it was announced that the Duke and Duchess of York were to separate following the publication of embarrassing photos of the Duchess on holiday with Texan Steve Wyatt; Princess Anne and Captain Mark Phillips announced they were to divorce in April; in June Andrew Morton's biography of the Princess of Wales, *Diana: Her True Story*, was published; even more humiliating were the 'Squidgygate' tape extracts of conversations between Diana and James Gilbey, which appeared in *The Sun* in August. The bad news didn't end there. In November the Queen was shown visibly shaken when her beloved home, Windsor Castle, was badly damaged by fire, and in early December Prime Minister John Major told the House of Commons that Charles and Diana were formally separating. As a final blow, *The Sun* leaked the transcript of the Queen's Christmas speech two days before it was shown. She issued a writ against the newspaper and eventually accepted an apology and a £200,000 donation to charity.

1993 In a sign of the times, the Queen and Prince Charles agreed to pay income tax and Buckingham Palace was opened to the public to help pay for the repairs to Windsor Castle. A reporter for the *Daily Mirror* also managed to infiltrate the Palace and published details of day-to-day royal life.

1994 Prince Charles admitted to his relationship with Camilla Parker Bowles in an authorized biography by Jonathan Dimbleby and accompanying television interview.

1995 In November, Princess Diana retaliated with her 'Queen of Hearts' television interview with Martin Bashir for *Panorama* on the BBC.

1996 The divorce settlements were finalized of both the Prince and Princess of Wales and the Duke and Duchess of York.

1997 Diana was killed in a car crash in a Paris tunnel on 31 August. Her funeral on 6 September followed a huge outpouring of public grief and was watched by over 32 million people in Britain alone.

The royal yacht *Britannia* was decommissioned in December. During nearly forty-four years of service it had travelled over a million miles on official and royal duties.

1999 Prince Edward married Sophie Rhys-Jones on 19 June. The couple were made Earl and Countess of Wessex just before the ceremony.

2000   The Queen Mother celebrated her 100th birthday on 4 August.

2002   The year began sadly with the deaths of Princess Margaret on 9 February and the Queen Mother on 30 March, just six weeks later. The Queen's Golden Jubilee celebrations, officially launched at the end of April, proved a surprise success and the show of support from the country emphasized the popularity of the monarchy. At the age of seventy-six, she became the oldest British monarch to celebrate fifty years on the throne.

2003   Lady Louise Mountbatten Windsor, the daughter of Prince Edward and Sophie, Countess of Wessex, was born on 8 November.

2005   Prince Charles and Camilla Parker Bowles were married on 9 April. The civil ceremony took place in the Guildhall in Windsor with a blessing at St George's Chapel.

2006   The Queen celebrated her eightieth birthday on 21 April.

2007   Elizabeth and Philip celebrated their 60th wedding anniversary. Queen Elizabeth became Britain's oldest ever reigning monarch. The record was previously held by her great-great-grandmother, Queen Victoria, who died in 1901 at the age of eighty-one.

    Their youngest grandchild, James, Viscount Severn, was born on 17 December to the Earl and Countess of Wessex.

2010   Princess Anne's son, Peter Phillips, and his wife, Autumn, welcomed the birth of their baby Savannah on 29 December – the Queen's first great-grandchild.

2011   Prince William married Catherine Middleton on 29 April in Westminster Abbey. They became the Duke and Duchess of Cambridge on their marriage and, in line with tradition, were also granted the titles Earl and Countess of Strathearn, and Baron and Lady Carrickfergus.

2012   The year of the Queen's Diamond Jubilee. Various events were staged to celebrate her sixty years on the throne particularly over the weekend of 2 to 5 June. The Olympics came to Britain with the Queen making a surprise appearance in a spoof James Bond sketch at the opening ceremony on 27 July. To top it all, Her Majesty then appeared to parachute into the Olympic stadium to roars of approval.

2013   George Alexander Louis, also known as Prince George of Cambridge, was born on 22 July. As the first child of Prince William and Catherine, he is third in line to the throne.

2014   On 8 September it was announced that the Duke and Duchess of Cambridge were expecting their second child.

God Save
Our Gracious
Queen

Even before she was crowned, the Queen always understood that hers was a long-term role, a job for life. At the cathedral service to mark her Silver Jubilee in 1977, the Queen declared, 'When I was twenty-one, I pledged my life to the service of our people, and I asked for God's help to make good that vow. Although that vow was made in my salad days, when I was still green in judgement, I do not regret nor retract one word of it.' She is a bridge between the very traditional reign of her grandfather King George V, the wartime monarchy of her father and the modern kingdom her son and grandson will one day inherit. The Queen, ably assisted throughout by Prince Philip, has kept the 'Firm' together and taken the royal family forward into the twenty-first century, while relaxing some of the boundaries that have kept the royal family at a distance for so long. 'She has let a little daylight in,' said royal documentary maker Michael Cockerell, 'but the magic is still there.'

At an honours investiture ceremony, the Queen was particularly impressed by a soldier to whom she was giving an award for gallantry. When she commended him for his bravery, he answered simply, 'It's just the training.'

She replied, 'I have a feeling that in the end, probably, the training is the answer to a great many things. You can do a lot if you're properly trained. And I hope I have been.'

Party Like a Princess

On VE day the Queen, then still Princess Elizabeth, had a glimpse of royalty as others see them. On 8 May 1945, the teenage princesses joined their parents and Prime Minister Winston Churchill on the balcony of Buckingham Palace to greet the jubilant crowds below, cheering and celebrating the announcement of Victory in Europe.

Later, wearing her ATS uniform with cap pulled down over her face to provide a degree of anonymity, the future queen slipped out into the streets with her sister and fourteen others to join the festivities. Margaret Rhodes, the Queen's cousin, was with them and describes how they linked arms to dance the conga, the Lambeth Walk and the hokey-cokey. Back at the palace they joined in the chants, 'We want the King; we want the Queen!' and cheered with the crowd when their parents appeared. The next night Princess Elizabeth wrote in her diary, 'Out in crowd again – Trafalgar Square, Piccadilly, Pall Mall, walked simply miles. Saw parents on balcony at 12.30 a.m. – ate, partied, bed 3 a.m!'

The princesses and their cousin again joined the revellers thronging the streets to celebrate the announcement of Japan's surrender and VJ day. Elizabeth wrote, 'Whitehall,

Mall, St J St, Piccadilly, Park Lane, Constitution Hill, ran through Ritz. Walked miles, drank in Dorchester, saw parents twice, miles away, so many people …' and the next night, '… congered into house [Buckingham Palace]… sang till 2 a.m. Bed at 3 a.m!'

On this last night, the princesses were recognized, but after a police officer warned, 'the princesses wish to be treated as private individuals,' they were not bothered by anyone.

A Royal Performance

Pageants, celebrations, special performances; the Queen's heart must sometimes sink at the thought of the 'entertainment' in store for her that day. The consummate professional, of course, she smiles politely and asks all the right questions, but occasionally there is a glimpse of what she really thinks.

To support the Venice in Peril Fund, a special screening of Visconti's *Death in Venice* was organized. John Julius Norwich was hosting the event and seated between the Queen and Princess Anne. A few minutes after the film had started, Norwich heard the Queen sigh, and then a little later she sighed again. 'It was a long sigh,' he said – and a long film. Over two hours and many sighs later the lights went on. The Queen turned and flashed a bright smile, 'Well, that was a bit gloomy, wasn't it?' Norwich explained, 'She was trying to put me at ease. She could sense my discomfort.'

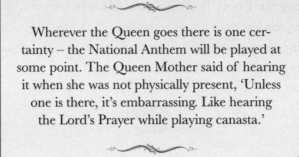

Wherever the Queen goes there is one certainty – the National Anthem will be played at some point. The Queen Mother said of hearing it when she was not physically present, 'Unless one is there, it's embarrassing. Like hearing the Lord's Prayer while playing canasta.'

Not surprisingly, Prince Philip can be less tactful. Tom Jones being one of the particularly unlucky targets for the Prince's derision over the years.

'What do you gargle with – pebbles?' Philip asked the singer after the 1969 Royal Variety Performance. Thinking further the next day, the Prince added, 'It is very difficult at all to see how it is possible to become immensely valuable by singing what I think are the most hideous songs.'

And he does not seem to have revised his opinion. While attending a small-business lunch, and in response to a comment about how hard it is to make a fortune in Britain, the Prince asked, 'What about Tom Jones? He's made a million and he's a bloody awful singer.'

The Queen also enjoys some acts more than others. After hearing the Everly Brothers singing 'Cathy's Clown' in the sixties, the less than impressed monarch turned to a lady-in-waiting accompanying her and admitted that she thought, 'They sound like two cats being strangled.'

The Queen and Prince Philip have sat through rather a lot of Royal Variety Performances, Her Majesty a total of thirty-seven. In recent years the Queen has alternated attendance with Prince Charles and in 2014 the pleasure passed to the younger Duke and Duchess of Cambridge. It is a tradition that the royals meet performers backstage after the show.

Meeting Tommy Cooper one year, the comedian asked the Queen if she minded him asking her a personal question.

'No,' Her Majesty replied. 'But I might not be able to give you a full answer.'

'Do you like football?' asked Cooper.

'Well, not really,' the Queen admitted.

'In that case, do you mind if I have your Cup Final tickets?'

> 'Are we going to need earplugs?' the Prince enquired after being told that Madonna was going to be singing the *Die Another Day* Bond theme in 2002.

Attending the 73rd Royal Variety Performance in 2001, Prince Philip made no secret of his opinion when he muttered loudly, 'I wish he'd turn the microphone off!' during Elton John's set.

It was not the only time that year that the Prince was rather insulting to the singer-songwriter, a near neighbour of the royal couple as he also owns a house in Windsor. On hearing that Elton John had sold his Watford Football Club-themed Aston Martin, Prince Philip said, 'Oh, it's you that owns that ghastly car is it? We often see it when driving to Windsor Castle.'

Celeb Spotting

The royal information feed was obviously not working properly when the Queen met guitar legend Eric Clapton at a Buckingham Palace Reception in 2005. She asked him politely, 'Have you been playing a long time?'

The Queen has been known to occasionally muddle people up. She once confused the Labour leader Michael Foot with the comedian Ken Dodd but charmingly apologized for the mistake. Foot afterwards remarked that the monarch had a 'surprisingly mirthful manner'.

On coming upon historian Andrew Roberts giving Kate Middleton a lesson on the history of the monarchy shortly before her wedding to Prince William, the Queen was convinced he was one of the Palace butlers.

> When introduced to artist Tracey Emin at the Turner Contemporary Art Centre in Kent in 2011, the Queen asked, 'Do you show internationally as well as in Margate?'

Veteran comedian Norman Wisdom made the Queen chuckle when he collected his knighthood in 2000. He performed one of his trademark trips as he walked away. 'I couldn't resist it,' he said later.

Trying to put Sharon Osbourne at ease after the television personality had sworn in front of her, the Duchess of Cornwall revealed, 'It's quite all right, we curse quite a lot around here.'

A year after the film *The Queen* had been released, for which Helen Mirren won an Oscar for her portrayal of Elizabeth II, the actress was at Ascot and the Queen invited her to the royal box for tea. The film depicted the royal family's response in the difficult days following the death of Princess Diana, widely regarded as a make-or-break moment for the monarchy. Afterwards, Helen Mirren said that she was very touched to be asked, commenting, 'I wouldn't have been invited to tea if she had hated the film.'

This was not the first time the Queen had met an actress who had portrayed her. After *A Question of Attribution*, the Alan Bennett story of Soviet spy and Palace art restorer Sir Anthony Blunt, hit the stage in 1991, she was introduced to Prunella Scales, who had played her part. When the actress bowed to her in a receiving line the Queen joked, 'I expect you think I should be doing that to you.'

In 2013, when presenting the Queen's Gold Medal for Poetry to John Agard, she couldn't help chuckling when she saw the figure of a naked woman that decorated the back of the medal and consequently the back of her own head, which appeared on the front.

Royal Jamborees

In 1977, Silver Jubilee fever gripped the country. Festivities began on Monday, 6 June, the Queen's official birthday. That night she stood on Snow Hill in Windsor Great Park ready to light the beacon that was the sign for a series of others across the country to be lit, just as they had been in the days of the Armada. Pyrotechnics expert and pageant master Major Sir Michael Parker had worried that the huge beacon would not light fast enough, so he had packed it with fireworks and positioned a Royal Signals major next to a detonator. Unfortunately, the soldier pressed the detonator too soon and the bonfire burst into flames.

'I can't think why you bothered to ask me [to do it],' the Queen laughed.

There were then problems with the sound system, and a deafening firework mortar went off instead of a flare. 'Your Majesty,' said Sir Michael, 'I'm afraid it's all going terribly wrong. In fact everything that could possibly go wrong is going wrong.'

Smiling broadly, the Queen replied, 'Oh good. What fun!'

In his diary, the late Earl Mountbatten recalls that during the Silver Jubilee thanksgiving service at St Paul's in 1977 the Queen had at one point looked very cross and worried. Asking her afterwards what had been the matter, the Queen replied, 'I was just thinking how awful it would be if (Idi) Amin [the former despotic president of Uganda] were to gatecrash the party and arrive after all.' In response to Mountbatten's further enquiry as to what the Queen would have done if this had happened, the Earl notes, 'She had decided she would use the City's Pearl Sword, which the Lord Mayor had placed in front of her, to hit him hard over the head with.'

The Golden Jubilee in June 2002 saw the staging of the 'Party at the Palace', which began with Brian May of the band Queen performing 'God Save the Queen' as a guitar solo on the roof of Buckingham Palace. At the end, in an unprecedented move, the royal family joined the stars of the show on the stage. Prince Charles led the thanks to the Queen for her fifty years on the throne. 'Your Majesty,' he started. 'Mummy …'

A CD of the 'Party at the Palace' concert sold 100,000 copies in its first week and made the Queen the first member of the royal family to be presented with a gold disc by the record industry.

As a royal couple, even wedding anniversaries become public events. 'I think everybody really will concede that on this, of all days, I should begin my speech with the words "My husband and I",' the Queen said at her 25th wedding anniversary celebration in 1972.

The 2012 London Olympics opening ceremony was a spectacle to remember. After seeing the Queen appear as perhaps the ultimate Bond girl, who could ever doubt her sense of humour?

Director Danny Boyle later revealed they had wanted to find a different way to introduce the monarch and national anthem and came up with the idea of the Bond sketch. They had fully expected to cast an actress to play the part of the Queen and wrote to the Palace, as protocol dictates, to ask for permission. To their surprise, Danny Boyle explained, 'They came back and said, "We're delighted for you to do it, and Her Majesty would like to be in it herself," and the surreal thing, "she would like to play herself".'

When it came to filming, it was the Queen who suggested she should say something and who came up with the lines. 'We started shooting and she turned round and she said her lines beautifully.'

The Queen's role in the spoof was such a closely guarded secret that even Princes Charles, William and Harry hadn't known about it. Like the rest of us, they watching in shocked surprise, before roaring with laughter.

A Thoroughly Modern Monarch

No stranger to technology, back in 1976 the Queen was the first head of state to send an email. She has since joined Facebook in November 2010, with a page called 'The British Monarchy'. It has received almost 1.5 million 'Likes' to date and features royal news, photos, videos and speeches. However, there are limits and it is not possible for other users to 'poke' the royal family.

Both the Queen and Prince Philip are enthusiastic 'Googlers', sharing any interesting finds with one another. When they visited the London headquarters of Google in 2008, they were shown a YouTube clip of the 'Laughing baby' and were soon laughing along. 'Lovely little thing, isn't it?' the Queen commented to Philip. 'Amazing a child would laugh like that.'

Upon being congratulated on writing her own diary in the old-fashioned way using pen and paper rather than word processor, the Queen declared, 'Well I can't write any other way.'

The Queen has made light of her daily jottings: 'It's not really a diary like Queen Victoria's ... or as detailed as that. It's quite small ... It's just like scrubbing your teeth.' The diary's contents will not be made public until after her death and close friends have speculated that it may contain some of the sharp observations and witty asides that are the Queen's forte in private.

In a year when photobombing became something of a national obsession, no one could have expected that Her Majesty the Queen would decide to join the craze. Picture the scene. It was July 2014 and a sunny day in Glasgow, where the Commonwealth Games were taking place. Jayde Taylor, a young Australian hockey player, paused to take a selfie with teammate Brooke Peris, unaware that she was being photobombed by a rather unlikely figure. Dressed in green, complete with feathered hat, the Queen stood smiling broadly at the camera through a chain link fence. She was obviously completely aware of what she was doing and thoroughly enjoying the joke.

And that isn't the only occasion when the Queen has dabbled with photobombing. During a BBC News broadcast the two presenters, live on air, were surprised to discover the figure of the Queen approaching the glass screen that separated them from the busy newsroom behind. Clad in bright turquoise, the Queen took centre stage surrounded by BBC staff keen to follow the royal progress, while the presenters struggled to regain their composure and control of the programme.

The Queen has also left her mark in space. On their return home from the first moon landing in 1969, the Apollo 11 astronauts left behind on the moon's surface a microfilmed message from the Queen. It said, 'On behalf of the British people I salute the skill and courage which have brought man to the moon. May this increase the knowledge and well-being of mankind.'

At
Home ...

No one can doubt the Queen's strong sense of duty, and her finely honed notion of what's right and proper seems to have developed at an early age. Ever the responsible older sister, she advised Princess Margaret when they were still children, 'If you see someone with a funny hat, Margaret, you must not point at it and laugh.'

Sometimes this polite formality can mask the Queen's sense of fun, although the slightly mischievous twinkle in the royal eye shows it's still there. And that's despite the weight of her full title, 'Her Majesty Elizabeth the Second, by the Grace of God, of the United Kingdom of Great Britain and Northern Ireland, and of Her Other Realms and Territories Queen, Head of the Commonwealth, Defender of the Faith', which, you have to admit, demands a great degree of dignity from its holder.

As the actress Helen Mirren, who played the part of Queen Elizabeth II to great acclaim, observed, 'To be that consistent for that long is amazingly comforting. It shows such reliability. She has never lurched in one direction or another. It is self-discipline, which I think comes from within rather than imposed from outside.' And it is while efficiently going about her day-to-day duties as sovereign that the Queen's humour can be seen, in the private looks and laughter shared with Prince Philip and other members of the royal party, and in her very public delight at the right occasion.

Concerning her realm, she is singularly well informed on all matters, although she has in the past confessed that 'the British Constitution has always been puzzling and always will be.' But it is perhaps a knowledge of the country's people rather than its political workings that has equipped her so well for her long reign. No doubt such expertise has been acquired over a lifetime of 'away days', as she and Prince Philip call their visits to cities and small villages throughout the UK, as well as meeting the thousands of guests who attend the regular garden parties hosted at Buckingham Palace.

'She spends so much time meeting people that she has an understanding of what other people's lives are like in Britain. I think she understands what the normal human condition is,' said Charles Powell, who witnessed the Queen in action when working as private secretary to both Margaret Thatcher and John Major. Others who have met her remark on her ability to speak to anyone on any level, whatever their background.

Strike a Pose

The Queen knows that being photographed by professionals and amateurs alike is part of the job description, and after so many years' practice she knows exactly how to make the best of any photo opportunity. She dresses to stand out from the crowd, choosing bright, distinctive colours: 'If I wore beige, nobody would know who I am.'

The Queen is careful to use a transparent umbrella in the rain so she can still be seen and she has a number of different ones, all edged with a band of colour selected to match her outfit. She is also very aware of camera angles and how to avoid potential embarrassment. When opening a British Council exhibition of Lucian Freud nudes in Norway she told an aide that she had been very careful to make sure 'I was not photographed between a pair of those great thighs.'

On that same trip a curator asked the Queen, 'Haven't you been painted by Lucian Freud, Ma'am?' The Queen smiled and replied, 'Yes, but not like that.'

When Freud painted her portrait in 2001 he was said to have had 'a whale of a time with the Queen', according to his friend Clarissa Eden. It took several sittings and staff became used to the sight of Her Majesty mid-morning, racing down a corridor in full regal regalia, complete with ballgown and tiara, late for her appointment with the artist.

Princess Margaret said of her sister, 'The Queen is the only person who can put on a tiara with one hand while walking down stairs.' Her skill obviously extends to running in a tiara.

> While unveiling a sculpture of Prince Philip, Prince Charles announced, 'I now complete the process of helping my father to expose himself.'

Gracious Hosts

The Queen favours the personal touch. When expecting guests, she always inspects their rooms herself. She also oversees arrangements for banquets and official dinners. However, once through the door, some guests show no inclination to leave the royal presence and the family have developed a code to get rid of guests who overstay their welcome. They will call for a butler and ask if the guest's car has arrived. The butler will 'check' and then return with the news that indeed the car is waiting.

Prince Philip has a reputation for not suffering fools gladly and when he hosts a private supper he prefers to set the topic for discussion at the table. Apparently, the secret is for guests to call his office in advance to check which subjects are currently interesting the Prince. They can then make sure they know just enough to keep the conversation flowing and not appear ill-informed but not so much that they outshine or out-talk their host.

While attending a lunch with the Queen at Windsor, one guest was struggling to be heard against the noise of aeroplanes flying overhead on their way to Heathrow. After the first disruption the Queen remarked, 'Boeing 747'. Minutes afterwards, another flew across. 'Airbus,' she said. Throughout the lunch she continued to identify every plane that passed over.

At a reception at Buckingham Palace one of the guests arrived late and missed his allotted place in the queue of diplomats waiting to be introduced to the Queen. Not wanting to lose the opportunity of sharing a few words with Her Majesty, he pushed in among the guests who were still waiting in line. But when he finally reached the Queen he was met with nothing more than a cold stare and the firm arms of officials who led him away. He should have known that upsetting the time-honoured British tradition of orderly queuing would fail to impress.

Prince Philip's outspoken, sometimes politically incorrect, remarks have got him into hot water from time to time. His comment made in an address to the General Dental Council in 1960 is still true today: 'Dontopedalogy is the science of opening your mouth and putting your foot in it, a science which I have practised for a good many years.'

- On meeting Sir Michael Bishop, who was chairman of Channel 4 at the time, the Prince exclaimed, 'So you're responsible for the kind of crap Channel 4 produces!'

- He also asked Simon Kelner, then editor-in-chief of *The Independent*, what he was doing at a press reception to celebrate the Golden Jubilee in 2002. On being told that Prince Philip had himself invited him, the Prince retorted snappily, 'Well you didn't have to come.'

- At a Buckingham Palace drinks party in 2000, seeing a group of female Labour MPs who were all wearing name badges bearing the title 'Ms', the Prince quipped, 'Ah, so this is feminist corner then.'

Royal Protocol

In an average year the Queen hosts more than 50,000 people at various garden parties, lunches, dinners, banquets and receptions held at Buckingham Palace.

When meeting the Queen there is a certain protocol to be followed, which on occasion must give Her Majesty no little cause for amusement, privately at least.

✦ When the Queen enters a room, everyone must stand, because she is never off-duty. The rule even applies to Prince Philip, although one must assume that the Queen relaxes it when they are alone.

✦ The Queen should first be addressed as 'Your Majesty' and afterwards as 'Ma'am', to rhyme with ham not harm, though it's back to 'Your Majesty' when she is leaving.

✦ Women should curtsey but men get away with a bow from the shoulders or nod of the neck on both meeting and saying goodbye to the sovereign. The Queen herself is said to be very relaxed about curtseying, commenting that it is 'not necessarily right for modern times'. The last person she curtseyed to was her father, King George VI.

✦ When departing, visitors used to have to walk backwards, but health and safety has done away with this requirement except for a few ceremonial occasions.

✦ At dinners, no one should begin eating before the Queen or continue once she has finished.

✦ One is not supposed to touch Her Majesty. If she offers a hand it is polite to take it, but for the briefest of touches rather than a full-on handshake.

Follow these rules and your meeting with the Queen should go without a hitch. But even those most trained in such matters can still slip up. Despite the general understanding that the Queen is not to be touched, there have been some notable breaches of this 'rule'.

At the G-20 London Summit in 2009, the Queen and Prince Philip formally met US President Barack Obama and his wife, Michelle, in their private apartments at Buckingham Palace, when royal etiquette was observed and gifts exchanged. Then later, at the evening reception for world leaders, Michelle Obama was photographed hugging the Queen, who reciprocated with an affectionate arm around the first lady's waist.

Or was it the Queen who touched first? Either way, the pair were seen standing together chatting, apparently comparing shoes and height – Michelle Obama is almost a foot taller and towered over the monarch. A Buckingham Palace spokesperson denied there had been a breach of protocol, saying, 'It was a mutual and spontaneous display of affection. We don't issue instructions on not touching the Queen.'

This was not the first time the Queen had been publicly touched. In a visit to Washington in 1991, sixty-seven-year-old great-grandmother Alice Frazier hugged the smiling Queen warmly when she visited her home, saying it felt like the natural thing to do. When former Australian Prime Minister Paul Keating put his arm around the Queen in 1992 he was labelled 'Lizard of Oz' by the tabloids, and when John Howard, his successor, was accused of repeating this gesture his office issued the statement, 'We firmly deny that there was any contact whatsoever.' President George W. Bush restricted himself to a sly wink to the Queen after mistakenly referring to her visit to the White House as occurring in 1776 rather than 1976. He later said that in response, 'She gave me a look only a mother could give a child.'

Meeting One's Subjects

When it comes to the honours system and the bestowing of awards, ceremonies are planned down to the tiniest detail. Around 3,000 medals are presented each year including

OBEs, CBEs and MBEs, all with a distinctive ribbon and leather box. There are twenty-two investitures at Buckingham Palace alone, with further ceremonies held in Edinburgh and Cardiff. The Queen has personally conducted over 540.

Normally, investiture ceremonies play out like a well-oiled machine. Before the ceremony begins, each person is told that the Queen will say a few words to them as she is attaching the insignia to their clothing, but that the exchange will be short. The Queen herself has said, 'One mustn't have a long conversation, obviously, because you'd never finish.' But with a sigh she admits, 'It doesn't always happen.'

On one occasion an unfortunate member of staff dropped the cushion holding the medals that had been carefully sorted and placed in the correct order in which they were to be handed out. Everyone looked on in horror. The ceremony was about to start.

Without missing a beat the Queen said, 'Just put them any way you can. I'll give them anything and you can sort it out afterwards.' She calmly carried on as if nothing untoward had happened and staff in a side office resolved the muddle and made sure everyone went away happily with the medal they were expecting.

> The Queen receives hundreds of letters a day, from congratulations on recent events in the Queen's life, to opinions on how the monarchy is run and even requests for advice on where to buy a corgi.

Queen Victoria began the tradition of holding a royal garden party to which select members of the public are invited. The Queen and Prince Philip now host three each year at Buckingham Palace plus another at Holyroodhouse in Edinburgh. Some 8,000 guests from all walks of life are invited to each one. The dress code is formal with women wearing stylish dresses or suits, usually combined with hats and gloves, and men in lounge suits, morning dress or uniform. It should be noted that the Queen only wears hats in the daytime, never after 6 p.m. Bands play and a final rendition of the national anthem signals the party is ending.

The garden parties are usually very civilized affairs although there have been some surprises over the years.

At one of the Buckingham Palace parties in 2003, a £100 wager with his brother led seventeen-year-old schoolboy Barney Keen to drop his trousers. He proceeded to race across the lawn, darting between guests while slapping his naked backside and yelling 'Wahey!' Eventually two Yeomen of the Guard crossed pikes to bar his progress whereupon police officers escorted him away. The Queen politely turned her back but is said to have found the incident amusing, his embarrassed parents rather less so. The youngster afterwards wrote a letter of apology and said he was sorry for the prank.

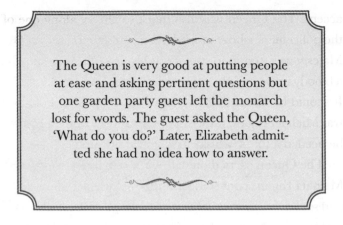

The Queen is very good at putting people at ease and asking pertinent questions but one garden party guest left the monarch lost for words. The guest asked the Queen, 'What do you do?' Later, Elizabeth admitted she had no idea how to answer.

Breaching the Battlements

One of the Queen's more notorious meetings with one of her subjects was very definitely not planned and must have been quite a shock, although she carried it off with an impressive level of cool. In the early hours of the morning on 9 July 1982, the Queen woke with a start to find a strange man with a cut hand, dripping blood onto the end of her bed. He was Michael Fagan, then thirty-two and unemployed. At the time there were reports that he had sat on the Queen's bed while she chatted to him but these have since been denied. The Queen managed to leave her bedroom to get help when Fagan asked for a cigarette. Historian Sally Bedell Smith wrote that the Queen later told friends the story, including a chambermaid's startled reaction, 'Bloody 'ell Ma'am, what's 'e doin' 'ere!' perfectly mimicking the girl's Yorkshire accent. The Queen was also quick to chivvy along one of the policemen, whose immediate reaction upon seeing Her Majesty was to stop to straighten his tie. 'Oh come on. Get a bloody move on,' she reportedly told the overawed officer. It should be noted that footman Paul Whybrew thought it was Michael Fagan, rather than the Queen, who looked like he needed a tot of whisky to calm his nerves.

The Queen carried on with the day's duties as planned. Michael Fagan spent some months in a psychiatric hospital and security measures at the royal palaces were re-evaluated and tightened.

Princess Anne showed her mother's strength of character during a failed kidnap attempt in March 1974. Ian Ball, a twenty-six-year-old who suffered with mental health problems, ambushed Anne's car in the Mall. He asked her to 'come with me for a day or two,' explaining this was because he wanted £2 million.

The Princess famously retorted, 'Not bloody likely!' and then added, 'And I haven't got £2 million,' before niftily escaping from the car. She was afterwards commended by Prime Minister Harold Wilson for her bravery. Ian Ball was armed and during the encounter shot and wounded the Princess's driver, two police officers and a journalist.

On Politics

During her years as monarch the Queen has appointed twelve prime ministers to date, meeting with them regularly each week to discuss affairs of state.

> Winston Churchill 1951–1955
> Anthony Eden 1955–1957
> Harold Macmillan 1957–1963
> Alec Douglas-Home 1963–1964
> Harold Wilson 1964–1970 and 1974–1976
> Edward Heath 1970–1974
> James Callaghan 1976–1979
> Margaret Thatcher 1979–1990
> John Major 1990–1997
> Tony Blair 1997–2007
> Gordon Brown 2007–2010
> David Cameron 2010–

When her own children were small, she asked the prime ministers to come later in the evening for their weekly Tuesday meetings so she had time to read her children their bedtime stories first.

It has always been maintained that the Queen does not favour one politician or party over another. As Sir Godfrey

Agnew, former Clerk of the Privy Council, claimed, 'The Queen doesn't make fine distinctions between politicians of different parties. They all roughly belong to the same social category in her view.'

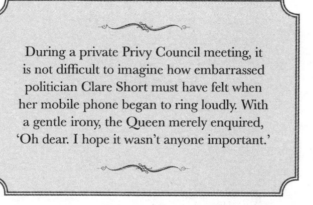

During a private Privy Council meeting, it is not difficult to imagine how embarrassed politician Clare Short must have felt when her mobile phone began to ring loudly. With a gentle irony, the Queen merely enquired, 'Oh dear. I hope it wasn't anyone important.'

The Queen and Prince Philip's nickname for the line-up of dignitaries who frequently greet them on official visits is the 'chain gang', a reference to the ceremonial robes, hats and chains often worn by mayors, sheriffs and their deputies.

In the late 1960s, the Queen was present at a meeting where Sir Edward Bridges, the cabinet secretary of the day, was coaching four ministers. Everything went wrong. They were kneeling on the wrong side and then crawled across to their proper positions knocking a book to the floor. The Queen picked it up looking absolutely furious. Later, the cabinet secretary returned to apologize to the Queen, who admitted, 'I nearly laughed.' Sir Edward realized that 'when she looked angry it was mainly because she was trying to stop herself laughing.'

Of the Commonwealth the Queen has said, 'It is easy enough to define what the Commonwealth is not. Indeed this is quite a popular pastime.'

And on the loss of the United States of America: 'We lost the American colonies because we lacked the statesmanship to know the right time and the manner of yielding what is impossible to keep.'

Prince Harry has said that 'Her knowledge of the Army is amazing for a grandmother; I suppose it is slightly her job.'

She is Queen of all she surveys; as Prince Andrew once said, 'The Queen's intelligence network is a hell of a lot better than anyone's in this palace. Bar none. She knows everything. I don't know how she does it. And she sees everything.'

Out and About

In recent years the Queen has increasingly asked to meet ordinary members of the public rather than dignitaries and visits have become more informal with the Queen smiling and chatting happily. There have also been some off-the-cuff remarks.

+ The Queen once reportedly said, 'Manchester, that's not such a nice place.'

+ Before visiting Kingston upon Hull in 1957, Her Majesty amended a speech written by an adviser to say, 'I am pleased to be in Kingston today,' rather than, 'I am very pleased ...' *The Times* had recently described the town as one of the 'few dogged bastions of republicanism' in the country.

+ On a walkabout in Scotland, a helpful observer commented that she looked just like the Queen, to which she quickly replied, 'How reassuring.'

And Philip, as usual, has also added his own tuppence worth.

- Prince Philip once asked a driving instructor in Scotland, 'How do you keep your natives off the booze long enough to get them through the test?'

- Also in Scotland, in August 1999, Prince Philip's verdict on a fuse box was that 'it looks as though it was put in by an Indian.' This was too great a gaffe even for the Prince and he later tried to correct his comment: 'I meant to say cowboys. I just got my cowboys and Indians mixed up.'

- On meeting Stoke-on-Trent's Labour MP Joan Walley at Buckingham Palace in 1997, Prince Philip voiced a one word condemnation of the city: 'Ghastly!' He had offered the same opinion of Beijing during a 1986 tour of China.

- According to Prince Philip, speaking at the opening of City Hall in 2002, 'The problem with London is the tourists. They cause the congestion. If we could just stop the tourism, we could stop the congestion.'

- And pity the poor car park attendant who failed to recognize His Royal Highness at Cambridge University in 1997, and in exchange received the pleasure of the Prince's annoyance, as the Prince dismissed him with 'You bloody silly fool!'

- In 2005 the Prince was overheard commenting at the engineering faculty at Bristol University, 'It doesn't look like much work goes on at this university.' It had been specially closed for the day in order that the Queen could officially open it.

At an engagement in Scotland, the royal car approached a line of people ready to receive the Queen and her party. Having emerged from the vehicle, the Queen looked back to notice that her then Lord Lieutenant of Lanarkshire, Lord Clydesmuir, was struggling to do the same, his long sword proving something of an anchor. After a few embarrassing moments as they waited to see if the Lord Lieutenant would unstick himself, the Queen decided to take the matter of introductions into her own hands. Advancing on the waiting people she said, 'My Lord Lieutenant appears to be having difficulty in getting out of the car, so I'd better introduce myself. I'm the Queen.'

Meeting a teenage army cadet who had lost nearly all of his sight in an IRA bomb attack, the Queen asked him how much he could see. Pointing to the bright uniform of the Middlesex and North-West London Army Cadet Force that the boy was wearing, Prince Philip chipped in, 'Not a lot, judging by that tie.'

When the Queen ascended the throne, her grandmother Queen Mary passed on two very practical pieces of advice: 'During public engagements one should sit down whenever possible and avail oneself of toilet facilities whenever the opportunity arises.' No doubt useful during her frequent 'away days' and meetings. Reports that she travels with her own loo seat are not true. It is only Prince Charles who has been known to do this.

> The Queen is said to dislike travelling by helicopter, no doubt agreeing with her mother who said, 'Travel by helicopter? I think the chopper has changed my life … rather as it did Anne Boleyn's.'

... And Abroad

People like seeing the Queen. The excitement of catching a glimpse of royalty brings out the crowds wherever she goes – even in staunch republics. Think of the rapturous greeting that awaits her whenever she visits the US and the interest that is focused on her every movement or wardrobe detail. State visits have always been a feature of the Queen's life. Just five months after her coronation she embarked on a mammoth six-month tour of the Commonwealth with Prince Philip, during which they covered some 43,000 miles. Over the course of her reign, the Queen has made over 261 official overseas visits to 116 different countries, which makes her far and away the most travelled head of state to date.

It's strange to think of a time when royal walkabouts were not an essential element of any royal visit. In fact, the first royal walkabout took place in 1970 during an official tour of Australia and New Zealand – hence the reason for the name. Then as now, they were seen as a relatively informal way for the Queen and Prince Philip to meet ordinary members of the public alongside the usual list of officials and dignitaries. The idea immediately caught on and walkabouts are now an expected part of any official visit. As the Queen herself quipped, 'I have to be seen to be believed.'

Walkabouts

Princess Anne was less keen on the idea at first and did not have fond memories of her first experience: 'At nineteen years old suddenly being dropped in the middle of the street, suddenly being told to pick someone and talk to them. Fun? No, I don't think so. A challenge.'

On a tour of Canada, visiting Saskatchewan, the Canadian minister Alvin Hamilton was concerned that the Queen had been on her feet all day and had not even requested a 'health break'. Her private secretary breezily replied that the Minister for Northern Affairs and National Resources need not worry, 'Her Majesty is trained for eight hours.' It's impossible not to wonder about the training sessions.

During one such state visit the Queen had to gently point out to an escort commander protectively blocking the crowd's view of the royal carriage: 'Actually, Captain, I think it's me they've come to see.'

Travelling in Royal Style

The Queen doesn't have a passport. As all British passports are issued in her name she has no need of one to travel. Every other member of the royal family has one.

As a fluent French speaker, the Queen does not need an interpreter when visiting French-speaking countries. Although this didn't stop Prince Philip complaining about French Canadians, remarking, 'Can't understand a word they say. They slur all their words.'

The Queen may have set off on her first Commonwealth tour on board SS *Gothic* but she sailed back along the Thames on board the newly commissioned royal yacht *Britannia*. From that time the yacht provided a real home from home for the royal family and represented freedom. It was somewhere they could hide away from public attention and really be themselves.

One may be travelling but one still likes the comforts of home. The Queen in an unguarded moment said, 'I'm so glad we've got the yacht with us this time. The last time we came here we had to stay in a guest house.' One is royal after all.

Douglas Hurd, the former Conservative Foreign Secretary, said, 'There was a magic about *Britannia* which had nothing to do with magnificence because she wasn't a magnificent ship.' He remembered the overseas tours on board the yacht as the 'most pleasant' of his Foreign Office career, also commenting, 'She was a homely ship in the proper sense.'

The Queen herself saw the weeks she spent on the yacht at the end of the summer as the one time she could be off-duty and fully relax. She told a Palace servant, 'I walk on at the end of a long summer season, I am absolutely exhausted and you won't see me for a couple of days … and at the end of a fortnight I can get off at Aberdeen with a spring in my heels, ready for another year.'

The choice of crew reflected the relaxed atmosphere. All were volunteer naval recruits and, as one of the officers explained, potential yachtsmen were asked only two questions at interview: 'Have you got a prison record; and have you got a sense of humour? And if they laughed at the first, there wasn't any need for the second.'

The Queen came to know the crew members personally and would always ask after them and their families. At the end of each day, the Queen liked to relax and literally kick off her shoes. Staff recall a lot of laughter and teasing during the gossip about the day's events and visitors. The Queen 'didn't miss a thing' and enjoyed the banter.

At *Britannia's* decommissioning service in 1997, the Queen was seen to wipe away a tear, one of the few occasions when the usually stoic monarch has let her emotions get the better of her in public.

Perhaps feeling nostalgic for *Britannia* as an oasis of calm, in 2002 Prince Philip announced to the Aircraft Research Association, 'If you travel as much as we do, you appreciate the improvements in aircraft design of less noise and more comfort – provided you don't travel in something called economy class, which sounds ghastly.'

Philip was also somewhat snappy with a local VIP meeting him from an airport who made the mistake of enquiring, 'What was your flight like, Your Royal Highness?'

'Have you ever flown in a plane?' HRH enquired. On being told, 'Oh yes, sir, many times,' Prince Philip replied, 'Well it was just like that.'

When making state visits the Queen has to have clothes for every eventuality, which means a choice of at least three outfits per day plus a set of mourning clothes, just in case. Her 'travelling yeoman' makes sure the royal luggage arrives safely ahead of Her Majesty. Occasionally, there are hitches. In 1983, visiting the west coast of America for the first time, everyone had expected Californian sunshine and the Queen had an array of light silk dresses to match the weather. In the event they were met by the worst weather there for decades and it rained non-stop. Every shot showed the Queen wearing the same raincoat until Princess Margaret was prompted to suggest her sister might consider buying a new coat.

In Nigeria once, the Queen's hosts were so concerned that she should not feel the heat, they cranked up the air conditioning to such a degree that her dresses froze on their hangers.

Visitors staying with the Queen often remark on how solicitous and even motherly she can be. She certainly displayed this caring side when she heard that journalist John Harrison's wife had gone into labour and he was not going to be able to get home in time for the birth after covering a royal tour of Canada. The Queen acted decisively, telling staff, 'That won't do at all. Let him fly home with me on the royal flight.' He did and successfully made it to the birth of his son, Paul. The Queen sent a message of congratulations to the couple. All she requested in return was that the journalist write nothing about the return flight, a pact that Harrison was happy to uphold.

Models of Diplomacy

As representatives of the UK, the royal couple have worked hard to ease diplomatic relations between countries over the years, travelling extensively. But despite the best intentions, their efforts have not always run smoothly. Prince Philip, for example, can hardly have endeared himself to the German people with his 1997 speech in Hanover. In a bizarre 'don't mention the war' scenario, he insisted on addressing Chancellor Helmut Kohl as 'Reichskanzler', a title previously held by Adolf Hitler.

In New Zealand, after the royal party was pelted with eggs by an anti-monarchy demonstrator, the Queen managed to laugh off the incident: 'I myself prefer my New Zealand eggs for breakfast.'

Not above enjoying a few moments of schoolboy humour, the Queen had to hide her face when she couldn't stop giggling after Jean Chrétien, Canada's former prime minister, swore because his pen had broken.

The Queen has never been one for confrontation or blank demands, preferring to make her wishes known in a softer manner. Discussing the Queen's state visit to the US in 1991, an adviser informed the Queen that she would be attending a baseball match and would be 'required to pitch the first ball'. Her initial demure response of, 'Oh really?' was followed by a pause and then, with a penetrating stare that spoke volumes, 'Are you sure?'

The Queen uses the phrase 'How fascinating' to mean a variety of different things, and often to show she disagrees with an opinion. It's all in the tone in which it is said.

Off the record the Queen can be scathing. Known to dislike pomposity and anyone who takes themself too seriously,

Her Majesty once described one such 'self-made toff' as a 'ghastly little crawler'.

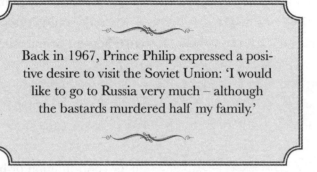

Back in 1967, Prince Philip expressed a positive desire to visit the Soviet Union: 'I would like to go to Russia very much – although the bastards murdered half my family.'

Hearing President Kennedy's wife, Jacqueline, complain of the pressures of public duty on tour as the first lady, the Queen passed on a tip, 'One gets crafty after a while and learns how to save oneself.'

Usually the model of diplomacy, the Queen sounded less than impressed on a visit to Niagara Falls in Canada when she remarked, 'It looks very damp.'

The Queen's state visit to the US in 1991 began with an official welcome on the lawn of the White House by the then President George H. W. Bush. After a few words from the President, the Queen was then to deliver her own short address. However, the President was a rather tall man, and when the Queen took the podium the only part of her that was visible was her purple and white striped hat, poking up behind the microphone. It was all the world's media could talk about. Exercising her characteristic good humour, the following day she began her speech to the joint houses of Congress: 'I do hope you can see me today from where you are.' The American politicians responded with raucous applause.

Prince Philip on Tour

Famous, or infamous, for the occasional ill-judged comment, Prince Philip seems never more gaffe-prone than when travelling abroad. Maybe he misses the comforts of home and is more than usually sharp-tongued? He was very quick to snap at BBC journalist Caroline Wyatt, 'Damn fool question!' All she had asked was whether the Queen was enjoying her stay in Paris in 2006. To be fair to the Prince, he is very equal in his disapproval and many people comment upon how charming and funny he is. His criticisms are usually accompanied by a telling twinkle in his eye.

Canada:

'We don't come here for our health. We can think of other ways of enjoying ourselves,' a grumpy Prince Philip pointed out in 1976.

Thailand:

After accepting an award for conservation in 1991, Prince Philip said, 'Your country is one of the most notorious centres of trading in endangered species in the world.'

The Cayman Islands:

'Aren't most of you descended from pirates?' he asked in 1994.

Nigeria:

He is reported to have commented to the president, 'You look like you're ready for bed,' presumably a reference to the head of state's formal white robes.

China:

'If you stay here much longer, you will go home with slitty eyes,' was the Prince's warning to twenty-one-year-old British student Simon Kirby studying in China in 1986.

Papua New Guinea:

'You managed not to get eaten then?' he asked another rather surprised British student who was trekking there in 1998.

Australia:

In 2002, he politely asked an Aboriginal leader in Queensland, 'Do you still throw spears at each other?'

Hungary:

In a reference to his opinion of Hungarian food, Prince Philip accosted a British tourist in Budapest in 1993 and announced, 'You can't have been here that long – you haven't got a pot belly.'

Slovenia:

'Tourism is just national prostitution. We don't need any more tourists. They ruin cities,' he told a university professor who in 2008 expressed a desire to attract more visitors to the country.

NASA:

The Prince was also less than impressed by the US Apollo space programme, dismissively stating, 'It seems to me that it's the best way of wasting money that I know of. I don't think investments on the moon pay a very high dividend.'

Many books have been written and websites created devoted to the Prince's gaffes, or 'Philipisms'. But he remains undeterred and has been heard to comment, 'I rather doubt whether anyone has ever been genuinely shocked by anything I have said.'

To the people of Tanna, an island in Vanuatu in the Pacific, Prince Philip is no mere mortal, but a god. An ancient island legend tells the story of a pale son of a mountain spirit who sails the world in search of a powerful wife. The myth somehow became associated with Prince Philip and, after a royal visit to Tanna in 1974, he was presented with a traditional club as a sign of respect. The islanders even mark the Prince's birthday with a ceremonial feast. Anthropologists call the Prince Philip Movement a cargo cult and it is seen as preserving ancient indigenous culture while absorbing aspects of the modern world. The Prince himself has been remarkably silent as to his opinion of it.

A
Family
Affair

The relaxed side of the Queen's character is perhaps most obvious when she is off-duty and with her nearest and sometimes not-so-dearest. Children, grandchildren, cousins, aunts, uncles, in-laws and mothers; births, deaths, marriages, divorces and scandals: the royal family is livelier than any soap opera. However, the genuine warmth and affection that she holds for her close family is obvious to all, and in their comments and stories about her it is clear the feeling is reciprocated. It is also her family who are the most frequent witnesses to the Queen's wickedest wit, and her grandchildren vouch for her talents as a mimic – politicians and prime ministers being a speciality.

Married to the twenty-one-year-old Princess Elizabeth in November 1947, Prince Philip has been at the Queen's side for official visits and state functions throughout her reign. At the coronation, Philip officially promised to 'become your liege man of life and limb, and of earthly worship …' and was indeed the first of her subjects to pay homage to the newly crowned Queen. Although afterwards he joked, 'Where did you get the hat?'

Elizabeth may be the ruler of the country, but at home, Philip is very definitely head of the family. He has regular meetings with each of his children individually, where he is said not to pull any punches when discussing the past months' achievements, plans, failings and general contribution to 'The Firm'.

This is a family which is happy to tease and be teased. No one is allowed to take themselves too seriously and they share a taste for practical jokes.

Princess Elizabeth

When they were young, Elizabeth and Margaret were not encouraged to mix very widely but an exception was made when it came to the Girl Guides, and in 1937 the 1st Buckingham Palace Company of Guides was formed. Soon after, the eleven-year-old Elizabeth requested that her younger sister, Margaret, also be allowed to join, adding, 'You see, she does so love getting dirty.' The resulting pack comprised around twenty Guides and fourteen Brownies, all carefully chosen, well-connected young girls. Their headquarters was a summer house in the gardens of Buckingham Palace, but the company closed with the outbreak of war.

The Queen acted in several of the pantomimes that were held in the Waterloo Chamber at Windsor Castle each winter. In 1941 she played the particularly dashing and aptly royal role of Prince Florizel, replete with curly wig, frilly cuffs and fetching breeches, in a production of *Cinderella*. Aladdin in 1943 was another lively performance. In truth, Princess Margaret probably enjoyed acting more than her sister but one of her performances had the audience laughing out loud, among them a young Prince Philip, who was beginning to take an interest in Elizabeth, to whom he had been introduced several years earlier.

In her book *The Final Curtsey*, the Queen's cousin Margaret Rhodes recalled holidays staying with her cousins at Balmoral. One year, the Grand Duchess Xenia, exiled sister of the last Tsar of Russia, was staying at Craigowan, a house on the Balmoral estate. Whenever Margaret and the young Princesses Elizabeth and Margaret were anywhere near Craigowan they would begin singing the Volga Boatmen's Song. 'We thought that the serenade would remind her of her homeland, but looking back I suppose our behaviour was less than sensitive, bearing in mind her tragic experiences during the revolution,' Margaret Rhodes writes.

> After their father's coronation as King George VI in 1937, Margaret asked if this meant that her older sister would have to be the next queen. When Elizabeth nodded, 'Yes someday,' Margaret commented, 'Poor you.'

The Happy Couple

The Queen is the only British monarch to have celebrated her diamond wedding anniversary and Prince Philip is now the oldest and longest-serving spouse of a British sovereign. Just before their marriage, the Queen's father, King George VI, granted Philip the title Duke of Edinburgh and allowed him to be called His Royal Highness. He has accompanied the Queen on all her Commonwealth tours and state visits overseas as well as countless public engagements at home. They make a formidable duo and there is no doubt that his support has been vital. The pair are often seen sharing a joke, laughing and swapping comments. That is not to say that it's always plain sailing. During a heated argument with Prince Philip in Australia during their Commonwealth tour in 1954, the Queen was filmed 'hurling shoes, threats and sporting equipment, and venting the sort of regal fury that, in another age, would have cost someone their head,' Robert Hardman has written. She later said, 'I'm sorry for that little interlude, but, as you know, it happens in every marriage.'

Upon his return from a four-month solo tour of the Commonwealth in 1957 – during which time he had grown an impressive array of facial hair – the Duke of Edinburgh was reportedly met by the Queen and a greeting party all sporting false ginger beards.

In his turn, and to mark the many weeks of their separation, Prince Philip wore a tie decorated with hearts.

> When asked for his advice, in 1997, on what made for a successful marriage, the Prince offered, 'Tolerance is the one essential ingredient ... You can take it from me that the Queen has the quality of tolerance in abundance.'

In 1992, Prince Philip was asked what he thought about his life. He replied, 'I'd much rather have stayed in the Navy, frankly.' Though this was perhaps more a comment on royal duties rather than marriage and family life.

After their diamond wedding anniversary in 2007, one of the Queen's advisers said of the royal couple, 'They are not physically demonstrative, but they have a strong connection. She still lights up when he walks into the room. She becomes softer, lighter and happier.' When they are apart,

Prince Philip rings his wife every evening to chat about the day's events.

When voted 'Consort of the Year' in February 2011 by the *Oldie* magazine, Prince Philip wrote them a letter, stating, 'There is nothing like it for morale to be reminded that the years are passing – ever more quickly – and that bits are dropping off the ancient frame. But it's nice to be remembered at all.'

More on the subject of age after his ninetieth birthday: 'I can only assume it is largely due to the accumulation of toasts to my health over the years that I am still enjoying a fairly satisfactory state of health and have reached such an unexpectedly great age.'

> The Prince made the following observation on men and women: 'If you see a man opening a car door for a woman, it means one of two things: it's either a new woman or a new car.'

The Children

Never one for false sentiment, the Queen complained, 'I'm getting fed up waiting for it to arrive', shortly before the birth of her granddaughter Princess Beatrice.

Prince Philip was even more blunt speaking about his daughter, Princess Anne, in 1970: 'If it doesn't fart or eat hay then she isn't interested.'

Of her own role following the birth of Prince Charles, Princess Margaret is quoted as saying, 'I suppose I'll now be known as Charley's aunt.'

And on family quarrels: 'In our family we don't have rifts. We have a jolly good row and then it's all over. And I've only twice ever had a row with my sister.' Tantalizingly, Princess Margaret did not reveal what those two arguments were about.

Princess Anne commented that she learned at an early age to accept that her mother would sometimes be away from home, occasionally for weeks at a time on overseas visits. She said that it was all part of 'the service life' and 'not a personal thing'. She added, 'As all mothers, she's put up with a lot and we're still on speaking terms, so I think that's no mean feat.'

When asked about preparation for life as a royal, Prince Charles said, 'You pick it up as you go along. You watch and learn … I learned the way a monkey learns – by watching its parents.'

The royals tend to live in traditional houses or established estates but when Prince Andrew and Sarah Ferguson married they built a new home in Sunninghill Park, which was completed in 1990. Not renowned for his tact, Prince Philip said of the house when he first visited, 'It looks like a tart's bedroom.'

The Queen Mother tried to be diplomatic about the house, which was often jokingly referred to as 'South York' after the ranch in the soap opera *Dallas*: 'If you'd spent most of your life on a warship you would not know about taste.'

Queen of the understatement as well as the realm, Elizabeth said of her *annus horribilis*, '1992 is not a year on which I shall look back with undiluted pleasure.'

The year had begun badly in January with the publication of embarrassing photos of Sarah, Duchess of York, on holiday with her Texan friend, Steve Wyatt, while shortly after came press pictures of Diana, sad and alone at the Taj Mahal, the famed monument to love and marriage. In March, the Duke and Duchess of York announced they were to formally separate and in April Princess Anne and Mark Phillips went a stage further and divorced on the grounds of his adultery.

Any hopes that the year would end quietly were dashed when a serious fire broke out at Windsor Castle on 20 November. The Queen's expression in news footage the next day revealed her desolation at the damage to the place she had always regarded as home. Alas, the year was not yet over and December saw the announcement that Charles and Diana were to separate. To top it all off, the Queen's Christmas speech was leaked to the press.

The Queen has since said of her family traumas, 'Like all the best families, we have our share of eccentricities, of impetuous and wayward youngsters, and of family disagreements.'

After meeting her future stepsons for the first time in 1998, Camilla admitted, 'I really need a gin and tonic.'

She needn't have worried; Prince Harry later said, 'She's a wonderful woman, and she's made our father very, very happy, which is the most important thing. William and I love her to bits. She's not the wicked stepmother.'

The Queen did not attend Prince Charles and Camilla's civil wedding ceremony on 9 April 2005 at the Guildhall in Windsor. At the time this decision attracted some press speculation about what the Queen really thought about the wedding. In reality, it was a reflection of the Queen's constitutional position and traditional faith rather than a sign of disapproval. However, her genuine happiness at the marriage was obvious in her warm speech later that day. She began by joking that she had an important announcement about the Grand National winner (Hedgehunter) and continued with the racing theme, saying of Charles and Camilla, 'They have overcome Becher's Brook and The Chair and all kinds of other obstacles [referring to the highest fences in the Grand National]. They have come through and I'm very proud and wish them well. My son is home and dry with the woman he loves. Welcome to the winner's enclosure.'

The Queen teased her then new daughter-in-law Sophie Wessex that she was 'the perfect royal', adding as a joke that a member of 'The Firm' should have the warmth of Fergie, the steadfastness of Mark 'Foggy' Phillips, and the poise of Princess Michael of Kent.

When William and Catherine announced their engagement in November 2010, both their families were delighted.

Prince Charles commented, 'They've been practising for long enough,' while his wife more effusively said, 'It's the most brilliant news. I'm just so happy and so are they. It's wicked.'

Asked why he had waited so long, William laughed, 'I didn't realise it was a race, otherwise I would have been a lot quicker.' He revealed, 'I was torn between asking Kate's dad first and then the realization that he might actually say no dawned upon me. So I thought if I ask Kate first then he can't really say no.'

Rather more seriously, William reflected, 'I wanted to give her a chance to see in and to back out if she needed to before it all got too much. I'm trying to learn from lessons in the past and I just wanted to give her the best chance to settle and to see what happens on the other side.'

What's in a Name?

> With the announcement that William and
> Kate's second baby was due in April 2015,
> bookies immediately opened the odds on
> names, with bets placed on everything from a
> possible Alexandra or Victoria to an unlikely
> Chardonnay if a girl, and James, Philip or
> even Elvis as a rank outsider if a boy.

The question of the royal family's surname became a thorny
one when Elizabeth ascended the throne in 1952. On the strong
advice of such heavyweights as Winston Churchill and her
formidable grandmother Queen Mary, the Queen agreed that
henceforward her children and future grandchildren should
all take the surname Windsor, not Philip's Mountbatten.

Philip was furious, ranting, 'I'm nothing but a bloody
amoeba … I am the only man in the country not allowed to
give his name to his children.'

Never really comfortable with this decision taken when
she was still a young and inexperienced monarch, the Queen
announced in 1960 that any of her direct descendants who
did not hold the title prince or princess would be called
Mountbatten-Windsor.

Given the family's taste for teasing, it is no surprise they are also fond of nicknames. As a small child, the Queen called herself 'Tillabet', later changed to 'Lilibet', an affectionate nickname still used by some members of her family and close friends. Princess Margaret was known as 'Baba'.

The Mitford sisters used to call the Queen Mother 'Cake' as a term of endearment, while the Duchess of Windsor nicknamed her 'Cookie', which was probably meant as an insult and alluded to her supposed resemblance to their Scottish cook. As a child, she was known as 'Merry Mischief'.

> When a young girl, the Queen Mother found herself running short of funds and sent her father a telegram asking for money: 'SOS, LSD, RSVP.' We are left to presume that she meant LSD to be an abbreviation of the pre-decimal currency (originating from the Latin '*librae*, *solidi* and *denarii*') rather than the hallucinogenic drug.

As a small child, Princess Elizabeth nicknamed her grandfather King George V 'Grandpapa England'.

Prince Charles and Camilla are rumoured to call one another 'Fred' and 'Gladys'.

At Timbertop School in Australia, where Charles spent two terms, he had the unflattering nickname, 'Pommy Bastard', but later described the experience as character building and said he had loved his time there.

Satirical magazine *Private Eye* refers to the Queen as 'Brenda'. In the past, the magazine has depicted the royal family as part of a soap opera, with suitable names to match. Prince Philip was 'Keith', Prince Charles was 'Brian', and Diana, Princess of Wales, was dubbed 'Cheryl'.

The younger royals have gamely kept up the tradition. Prince William admits to being called 'Wombat' as a child by his mother, Diana; this seems to have followed a visit to Australia when William was two, but 'Not because I look like a wombat. Or maybe I do!'

Prince William was known as 'Steve' to preserve some degree of anonymity when he was a student at the University of St Andrews. Prince Harry used to refer to himself as 'Spike', while Prince Charles, in his younger days, would sign himself into clubs as 'Charlie Chester'. Ever one for keeping it real, Prince Harry in his best man's speech at his brother's wedding repeatedly referred to the groom as 'dude'.

In the film *The Queen*, in which Helen Mirren plays Her Majesty, Prince Philip is shown on an evening at Balmoral calling his wife 'Cabbage'. Whether this is an authentic nickname we'll likely never know, but he is also said to talk about her fondly as 'Sausage'.

And on nicknames for Harry, William joked, 'Oh Ginger, whatever. You can call him whatever you want. Most of them ... a bit rude.' And when asked about phone calls or texts from his brother, William added, 'It usually means he's left something at home and I have to bring it for him ... He's a wild thing, all right.'

William and his wife, the Duchess of Cambridge, in their turn affectionately dubbed Prince George 'our little grape' before he was born. Now the royal family are said to call Kate 'MC', which stands for Mother Cambridge, and George 'PC', for Prince Cambridge.

> Members of the wider family have also acquired nicknames. Princess Alexandra is called 'Pud' because she was born at Christmas. Lady Helen Windsor is known as 'Melons' or 'Royal Raver'. Princess Michael of Kent has several nicknames, all along the same lines, and rather less affectionate – 'Princess Pushy', 'Princess Porky', 'Rent-a-Princess' and 'Our Val'. She was widely reported as saying, 'I'd go anywhere for a free meal.'

The Handbag

Have you ever wondered exactly what is inside the royal handbag? No outfit worn by the Queen is complete without an elegant coordinating bag adorning the royal arm. Launer of London has always made Her Majesty's bags in a range of different colours with slight variations of style. The Queen has no need of most of the usual handbag clutter such as passport, driving licence, travel cards or even credit cards and money.

Ever practical, the handbag is likely to contain reading glasses, mints, a fountain pen and tissues or handkerchief. It has also been suggested that she carries a mobile phone to text and speak to her family. And because she has been photographed taking them out, we know she carries lipstick and a compact mirror. Photos were published of the Queen reapplying red lipstick at the opening of the Commonwealth Games in July 2014, ending any question of whether it was a social faux pas to apply lipstick in public. According to royal historian Sally Bedell Smith, former first lady Laura Bush assured fellow guests at a Washington ladies lunch, 'The Queen told me it was all right to do it,' as she checked her lippy.

Actor Roger Moore's then wife Luisa once asked the Queen why she carried her handbag around with her inside Buckingham Palace. Her Majesty replied, 'This house is very big, you know.'

According to royal author Phil Dampier, the Queen is surprisingly superstitious and likes to keep a number of good luck charms with her, including tiny dogs, horses and miniature saddles; these are usually presents from her family and often on an animal theme. She also carries sweeteners in a small worn gold box that was a present from her sister, Margaret, and a photograph of Prince Andrew taken on his safe return from the Falklands conflict. More practically, the handbag frequently contains an S-shaped metal hook with plastic suction pads, which the Queen uses for convenience to hang the bag from a dining table.

Ladies-in-waiting are always on hand to carry the bulk of anything the Queen might need and a significant part of the handbag's importance lies in its use to send signals to staff. On walkabouts the way the Queen holds her handbag is crucial. If all is well, the handbag is held in the crook of her left arm. When she is ready to move on, the bag is dropped to the side significantly as a sign to one of her staff to step in to talk in her place as she walks away. Placed on the table at lunch or dinner it indicates the Queen is ready to leave in five minutes. And beware if the bag is placed on the floor. This shows Her Majesty is bored and wants to be rescued.

The Queen is well aware of the speculation surrounding the contents of her handbag and has been known to deliberately open it in clear view of press photographers so they can see inside. In April 2006 she also snapped it open to whip out a crisp ten-pound note for the church collection plate at St George's Chapel, Windsor, at a service celebrating her eightieth birthday.

Corgis, Dorgis, Spaniels and Labradors: The Royal Pets

D ogs of various breeds, horses, even racing pigeons: Her Majesty's affection for animals is well known and she has always kept a variety of pets, although cats never seem to feature in the retinue. In this the Queen is following a long family tradition and royal portraits from the seventeenth century onwards often include a favourite pug, corgi, spaniel or greyhound. Queen Victoria was so attached to her collie, Noble, that when he died he was buried at Balmoral, where his gravestone bears the inscription: 'Noble by name by nature noble too, Faithful companion sympathetic true, His remains are interred here.' King Edward VII's terrier Caesar was so much a part of the family that he was even included in the King's funeral procession, walking behind the coffin.

The Queen's first dog was a cairn terrier, a present from her uncle Edward, Prince of Wales, when she was just three years old. It was her father who introduced his young daughter to Pembroke Welsh corgis, the breed she is still associated with, when he brought home Dookie in 1933. Dookie was actually a nickname, a shortened version of the future king's own title, Duke of York. The young dog soon refused to answer to any other name, perhaps unsurprisingly given the fact that his pedigree name was the decidedly less catchy Rozavel Golden Eagle. Dookie was soon followed by Jane and later by her puppies Crackers and Carol.

When Princess Elizabeth was eighteen she was given her own corgi, Susan, from whom all her others are descended. The Queen has also introduced a new breed called dorgis, which are a cross between corgis and dachshunds, the result of breeding her own corgis with Princess Margaret's dachshund, Pipkin. At the moment, the Queen owns two corgis called Willow and Holly and two dorgis called Candy and Vulcan.

They are completely spoiled pooches, travelling everywhere with Her Majesty and enjoying the run of the palaces. So attached was she to Susan that she took the dog on her honeymoon. One can only imagine what Prince Philip thought of this. Perhaps he was inclined to be indulgent of his new bride as he is said to dislike the corgis' tendency to yap.

> When Princess Michael of Kent commented during a television interview that she would rather like to shoot the Queen's corgis, the monarch apparently retorted, 'They're better behaved than she is!'

Pampered Pooches

The Queen takes the welfare of her pets very seriously. The dogs sleep close to her apartment in raised wicker baskets to avoid draughts and are free to wander, occasionally sleeping in the royal bedroom. Whenever possible the Queen mixes their food and feeds them herself with chef-prepared fresh meat and gravy mixed with kibble. Steak, chicken, game and rabbit from one of the estates all feature. There is said to be a daily menu for the dogs' dinners, which are served promptly at 5 p.m. According to royal biographer and broadcaster Brian Hoey, the corgis wait for the royal command before they begin eating.

The Queen tries to make sure she's home for the birth of any litters and treats her dogs with homeopathic remedies when they are unwell. As a fan of homeopathy, her motto is very much if it's good enough for her it's good enough for her dogs. She also makes up Christmas stockings for the pets including treats and toys and is rumoured to remove noisy squeakers from cuddly toys herself when necessary.

> When snooker player Steve Davis visited the Palace he had the temerity to suggest that one of the corgis looked overfed. The Queen was not impressed and looked very cross, coldly replying, 'Corgis have small legs and they all look like that.'

During dress fittings at any of the palaces, the Queen always carries a magnet in order to pick up stray pins or needles that might injure one of the dogs.

It's no secret that the Queen's affection for her corgis is not entirely shared by the rest of the family. Prince Philip has been known to complain about the noise they make and he, along with Prince Edward, prefers Labradors. Prince Andrew and his daughters usually go for Norfolk terriers, while the Duchess of Cornwall is known to like Jack Russells. William and Kate have a black working cocker spaniel called Lupo who was a present from Kate's mother. Lupo is such a firm member of their family that he regularly appears in family photos, including the first official portraits with baby George.

Snap Happy

With a reputation for snappiness (and occasional incontinence), the Queen's dogs are not always popular with the staff. A ready supply of blotting paper and soda water is kept on hand to deal with any accidents. It is said that servants fed up with snappy corgis nipping their ankles have been known to retaliate with a quick blast from a soda siphon. The Queen is kept in blissful ignorance of the real reason why her pets are sometimes rather damp when they trot in to see her.

Upon discovering that one disgruntled member of staff was lacing her dogs' food and water with booze, the Queen was absolutely not amused. In 1999 Matthew King thought it was an entertaining prank to slip them whisky and gin then watch the corgis stagger tipsily around. The footman soon found himself demoted and lost various privileges that had gone with his job.

The Queen is not the most sympathetic to anyone who has the misfortune to upset the corgis and suffer the consequences. When two of the dogs nipped at a footman's heels causing him to trip, dropping a tea tray and painfully twisting his ankle, Her Majesty's primary concern was for her pets.

In 2005, designer Karl-Ludwig Rehse had a close shave: 'There were six or seven corgis waiting to be fed and I made the mistake of running down the corridor. One of them bit me and I looked down to see a small hole in my trousers and a trickle of blood. But when I went back to the Queen I felt obliged to apologize for my dishevelled appearance and I ended up saying, "I'm very sorry Your Majesty, but one of them bit me!"'

With so many dogs there is a tendency for them to form a pack and when other members of the family visit with their own dogs it is not unusual for fights to break out. The Queen does not hesitate to intervene when needed and in 2006 needed three stitches after breaking up a fight. William and Catherine were expressly asked not to bring Lupo, their black cocker spaniel, to Sandringham for Christmas 2013. This was to avoid a repeat of a previous family occasion when one of the corgis attacked Princess Beatrice's elderly Norfolk terrier, Max, who was so badly bitten he nearly lost an ear.

In keeping with her fondness for dogs of all kinds, the Queen has long been a patron of Battersea Dogs and Cats Home, although she has never been known to keep a cat as a pet. A pedigree Siamese kitten given to her as a present was duly passed on to one of the cooks.

Honoured Hounds

The kennels at Sandringham were established by King Edward VII in 1879 and the Queen still takes a personal interest in their running. She helps name the puppies born there and all have the Sandringham prefix as part of their official registration with the Kennel Club. Over the years there have been so many different dogs and litters of puppies that naming them all has required some imagination and humour. One litter of black Sandringham Labradors were called after various hats – Bonnet, Cap, Stetson, Trilby and Turban – while another all had names beginning with the letter D and featured Dilys, Dolphin and Drum. More recently, names were chosen from the Harry Potter books, with a particularly promising Labrador puppy called Gryffindor. The Queen also named two of her spaniels Bisto and Oxo, and called one of her racehorses Charlton after the famous footballing brothers Bobby and Jack. Her sense of fun in choosing her pets' names can be seen early on when as a child she called her corgi Jane's puppies Carol and Crackers because they were born on Christmas Eve.

Prince Philip named some of his own dogs after orchestral conductors and another litter after British cars of the time: Fiesta, Lagonda, Minor and Minx. Their mother had been called Mini.

The family's nickname for the cocker spaniels is 'the hoovers'.

The royal family's affection for their dogs and pets is reflected in the pet graveyard set in a quiet corner of the Sandringham estate. The Queen's beloved corgi Susan was buried there in 1959, her grave bearing the simple inscription, 'The faithful companion of the Queen'. The majority of Susan's descendants are also there, although Monty, who famously starred alongside his mistress in the James Bond sketch for the opening ceremony of the 2012 Olympics, is buried near to Queen Victoria's collie Noble at Balmoral, where he died.

While many of the graves carry the same affectionate epitaph as Susan's, some of the headstones reflect the dog's character. Sandringham Fern, a roan cocker spaniel, is described as a 'Tireless worker and mischievous character', while a black Labrador called Sandringham Brae is noted to have been 'A Gentleman Amongst Dogs'.

The wall around the cemetery is set with plaques commemorating other royal pets.

Not Just for Christmas!

As British sovereign making official visits abroad and welcoming state visitors to the UK, the Queen and her family are often given pets as presents, some rather exotic. President Tubman of Liberia gave Prince Philip a pair of pygmy hippopotami, which were soon given a home at London Zoo, while in 1956, Soviet leaders Bulganin and Khrushchev presented the young Princess Anne with a brown Syrian bear cub. But pity the Queen's Private Secretary Sir Martin Charteris, who was asked by his boss to look after a crocodile, a present for Prince Andrew. One assumes the Queen knew the ever-resourceful Sir Martin would rise to the challenge, and in the event he kept the reptile in his bathtub until a more suitable lodging could be found for it.

Other living gifts have included sloths and jaguars from Brazil, black beavers from Canada, two giant turtles from the Seychelles, a canary from Germany, a seven-year-old bull elephant called Jumbo from Cameroon, llamas and a large number of horses. The Queen's favourite Trooping the Colour horse was a present from the Royal Canadian Mounted Police. She was a black mare named Burmese and the Queen rode her for eighteen successive years, from 1969 to 1986, after which the horse retired. The Queen never replaced Burmese and has since ridden in Queen Victoria's phaeton carriage for the birthday parade.

As a child the Queen enjoyed playing with her collection of thirty toy horses, which she would carefully line up on the landing of her family's home at 145 Piccadilly, before she became heir to the throne following her uncle's abdication. Her favourite was a model pony with a brushable mane and tail.

Wildlife

Though not strictly 'pets', all 'the fishes royal' found in UK waters officially belong to the Queen as sovereign of the British Isles. A statute drawn up in 1324 during the reign of King Edward II remains valid today and states, 'Also the King shall have … whales and sturgeons taken in the sea or elsewhere within the realm.' This means that any 'fishes royal', which include sturgeons, porpoises, whales and dolphins, that come ashore or are caught within five kilometres of UK shores can be claimed on behalf of the Crown. In reality, if for instance a sturgeon is landed, it would be sold like any other fish, but as a gesture of loyalty to the monarch, the buyer requests the honour of it being accepted by the Queen.

Never one to keep his opinions to himself, on meeting three employees of a Scottish fish farm at Holyrood Palace in 1999, Prince Philip declared, 'Oh! You are the people ruining the rivers and the environment.'

The Prince also made his opinion of cats very clear when visiting a project for the protection of turtle doves in Anguilla back in 1965: 'Cats kill far more birds than men. Why don't you have a slogan: "Kill a cat and save a bird"?' Care for the environment has always been a major concern for the Prince, long before it became fashionable, and he has written a number of books on the subject. He is also a keen 'twitcher' and since 1987 has been Patron of the British Trust for Ornithology.

In a tradition dating back to the twelfth century, the British monarch can also claim ownership of all unmarked mute swans in open water. In practice, the Queen only exercises this right on specific stretches of the River Thames and its tributaries. She shares ownership with the Worshipful Company of Vintners and the Worshipful Company of Dyers, which were granted these rights by the Crown in the fifteenth century. At the time, swans were served as a delicacy at banquets where they made a particularly impressive centrepiece to the feast.

A Swan Marker is appointed to look after the Queen's swans and they take part in an annual Swan Upping ceremony along with the Royal Swan Uppers and the Swan Uppers of the Vintners and Dyers Companies.

The ceremony involves a five-day journey upriver in Thames rowing skiffs flying the appropriate flags and royal pennants. The Royal Swan Uppers wear traditional scarlet uniforms, and when a brood of cygnets is spotted a cry of 'All Up!' goes out as the skiffs row into position. On passing

Windsor Castle, oars are raised and 'Her Majesty, the Queen, Seigneur of the Swans' is saluted.

Swan Upping is not only a historic ceremony, it also serves a practical purpose. Cygnets are weighed and measured and all swans are given a health check. They are examined for signs of injuries, often caused by fishing lines and hooks, then ringed with identification numbers. Afterwards, the Queen's Swan Marker writes up a detailed report, which is vital for swan conservation. They also advise other organizations throughout the country on swan welfare and ecology.

Local school children are invited to watch the Swan Upping ceremony each year and on 20 July 2009 the Queen herself attended in person for the first time, becoming the first monarch and Seigneur of the Swans to do so for centuries. She took great pleasure in being able to combine her passion for wildlife with the traditional pomp and circumstance that go with the job.

Speaking at a World Wildlife Fund conference Prince Philip declared, 'If it has got four legs and is not a chair, if it has two wings and it flies but is not an aeroplane, and if it swims and is not a submarine, the Cantonese will eat it.'

A
Royal
Flutter

Elizabeth II reads the racing newspaper *Racing Post* avidly most mornings and servants know that any horse races must be recorded ready for her to watch when she returns home later in the day. While the Queen Mother was a patron of National Hunt racing, the Queen has always preferred the flat and never misses Royal Ascot.

The Queen and Queen Mum only ever owned one horse jointly and it was this horse, Monaveen, that gave the Queen her first taste of victory in 1949 when he won at Fontwell. Monaveen went on to other wins and raced in the Grand National but after a fall in the steeplechase at Hurst Park he was so badly injured he had to be destroyed. The Queen was said to be so upset by this that she decided to concentrate on flat racing, seeing it as less dangerous for the horses.

Ever mindful of her duties as monarch, left to her own devices Elizabeth's natural inclinations might lead her in a rather different direction. She has been quoted as saying, 'If it were not for my Archbishop of Canterbury, I should be off in my plane to Longchamp [the well-known race course in Paris] every Sunday.'

On For a Winner

Her sheer enjoyment and excitement at the races is obvious to any observer and never more so than when one of her horses is winning. Her gleeful exhilaration was caught on film by BBC cameras when Free Agent became her twentieth winner at the Chesham Stakes in 2008. The two-year-old colt broke through almost at the last moment and took the race conclusively by two-and-a-quarter lengths. Much to everyone's surprise the Queen jumped to her feet in excitement and punched the air triumphantly with a shout of, 'I've done it!' Her Bloodstock and Racing Adviser, John Warren, struggled to keep up with the monarch as she dashed away to greet her horse. 'It was a moment of real joy ... she raced to the paddock like she was twenty,' he said afterwards.

The Queen has wryly commented that owning a racehorse is much the same as fitting a tap to your pocket and she is not one of the front runners when it comes to buying the most expensive horses. Perhaps as a result, she has still not achieved her ambition of owning a Derby winner (she has come close at second and third), although she has won almost every other major race over the years, including the 1000 Guineas, the 2000 Guineas, the Oaks and St Leger.

It is a sign of her commitment and love of the sport that her racing manager and trainers are allowed to call her at any time on her private line. They also enjoy an unrivalled degree of informality in their dealings with Her Majesty. Richard Hannon, one of her trainers, once asked, 'Ma'am, do you speak Indian?' To which the Queen replied, 'No, I'm afraid I don't.' Hannon then commented, 'Well you ought to Ma'am. You ruled the place for long enough.'

Preferring to watch the races on television rather than with binoculars, the Queen will watch the action right up until the moment that the horses race past the royal box, at which point she'll hurry out of the television room and onto the balcony. Dignity and age are of lesser consideration during the manoeuvre and she can reach quite a speed as she gallops outside to see the winner take the line.

Traditionally, the journey from Windsor Castle to the racecourse at Ascot is taken by horse-drawn carriage. On one such occasion, according to the then royal footman Paul Burrell, the Queen had taken the open landau, accompanied by her husband and Prince Charles. Amid the cheers a cockney voice made itself clear. The Queen responded with a smile and a wave. 'What did he say?' asked Charles. The Queen replied, 'He said, "Gizza wave, Liz",' and broke out into hoots of laughter.

The Queen's racing colours are the same as those of her father and great-grandfather King Edward VII – a purple jacket with gold braid and scarlet sleeves worn with a black velvet cap with a gold fringe.

The Queen's diary is drawn up in draft eighteen months in advance with a final version confirmed six months ahead, but staff know that six days each year are sacrosanct and must remain free. Those are Derby day at Epsom and the five days of Ascot.

One question that is often asked is whether or not the Queen ever bets on her horses. To which the official answer is an emphatic 'Of course not!' There were constant rumours that the Queen Mother had a telephone account with one of the bookmakers, added to no doubt by her portrayal in satirical magazines and programmes such as *Spitting Image*. When one hack dared to ask her outright she simply laughed and said, 'You can't ask me that!' She didn't actually deny it, though, and anyone who saw the Queen or Queen Mum's excitement at the races would suspect that, while they may not place the bets themselves, there has never been a shortage of discreet friends or staff members to do it for them.

The one occasion when the Queen does admit to dabbling with betting is the traditional household sweepstake taken just before the Derby and drawn by the Queen. So, while her own horses are yet to take the honours, she has at least experienced the thrill of a sweepstake winner.

Sir Peter O'Sullevan, the famous racing commentator, has a story of when he tried to explain to the Queen why her favourite jockey, Lester Piggott, had been jailed in 1987. 'I told her all he'd done was merely deprive Customs and Excise of a small amount of tax revenue. She replied, tongue-in-cheek, "No. Lester has been very, very naughty."'

Game On

Princess Anne has inherited her mother's love of horses and is also a keen and accomplished horsewoman. She was European cross-country champion in 1971, riding Doublet, and a member of the British Equestrian team, winning silver medals in the European Championship in 1975 both individually and as part of the team. She also represented Britain in the 1976 Montreal Olympics and in 2012 was obviously very proud to present her daughter, Zara Phillips, with a silver medal at the equestrian events in Greenwich Park during the London Olympics.

'When I'm approaching a water jump, with dozens of photographers waiting for me to fall in, and hundreds of spectators wondering what's going to happen next, the horse is just about the only one who doesn't know I am royal,' Princess Anne said of her years of competitive riding.

Referring to her horsey reputation, Princess Anne said, 'When I appear in public people expect me to neigh, grind my teeth, paw the ground and swish my tail – none of which is easy.' She added, 'I'm not everyone's idea of a fairytale princess.'

Never the biggest fan of the press or public, after a series of equestrian events were held on her estate with its carefully managed organic grassland, Anne sardonically commented, 'And having the great British public tramping around is hardly organic.'

Princess Anne also voiced an opinion on another popular sport that many would share: 'Golf seems to be an arduous way to go for a walk. I prefer to take the dogs out.'

> Prince Philip is also fond of horses and riding but less enamoured of horse racing. He has been known to hide a radio in his top hat when attending Ascot so that he can listen to the cricket.

Prince Philip is, however, a big fan of polo, claiming in 1965, 'The only active sport which I follow is polo – and most of the work is done by the pony.'

The thrill of the sport has attracted his sons and grand-sons, too. Princes Charles, William and Harry are all keen players, undeterred by the odd knock. Although Prince William was less keen on the dangers of school sports: 'I gave up playing hockey when a friend of mine had his teeth knocked out. Put me off a bit.'

Prince Philip also relishes a challenge, although he is probably unlikely to repeat his 1985 feat when he drove a coach and four horses across Morecambe Bay in Lancashire when the tide was coming in. The seas there are known to turn very quickly and the Prince had to navigate swirling waves and dangerous quicksand to complete his mad dash.

As an ex-naval officer, it is no surprise that Philip is a keen sailor. He used to compete regularly at the Cowes Regatta and is Admiral of the Royal Yacht Squadron and the patron of many sailing clubs. Slightly less expected is his interest in tiddlywinks. He has awarded the 'Silver Wink' to the winner of the Inter-University Tiddlywinks Championship every year since 1961.

Pigeons and Prima Donnas

Less well known, and not altogether in keeping with most people's idea of royalty, is the Queen's interest in racing pigeons. In fact, Sandringham Lightning, one of the Queen's birds, came first in a section of the Pau race in 1990. Her family has a long association with the sport dating back to the 1880s when King Leopold II of Belgium presented them with their first racing pigeons. Elizabeth II is the royal patron of several pigeon racing societies including the Royal Pigeon Racing Association.

The Queen also enjoys cricket. The story goes that a new member of staff at Balmoral was more than a little surprised to come upon the monarch jumping up and down with delight exclaiming, 'I've won, I've won!' She had just heard that England's test cricketers had defeated the Australians.

As part of her royal duties, the Queen attends a wide range of other sporting fixtures, often presenting the winning trophies. She used to present the trophy to the winners of the

FA Cup Final but handed this task over to Prince William when he became President of the FA.

'Football's a difficult business and aren't they prima donnas? But it's a wonderful game,' the Queen observed while knighting Premier League chairman David Richards in November 2006.

While staying in the Highlands, the Queen and Prince Philip enjoy watching the Highland Games. At Braemar in 1982, the Queen found herself in a sticky situation. Congratulating shot put champion Geoff Capes, she shook his hand only to find their hands stuck fast together because of the resin he used for grip while competing.

Royals
in Residence

One of the great perks of being monarch is having a large number of different homes to choose from, conveniently placed throughout the realm.

The Queen privately owns Sandringham House in Norfolk, and Balmoral Castle, Craigowan Lodge and Delnadamph Lodge on the Balmoral Estate in Aberdeenshire. State-owned palaces include Buckingham Palace; the Queen's favourite bolt-hole, Windsor Castle; Clarence House, Kensington Palace, Wren House and St James's Palace in London; the Palace of Holyroodhouse in Edinburgh; and Hillsborough Castle in Northern Ireland. Other residences available to the Queen, if she so desires, include Hampton Court Palace, the Tower of London and the Palace of Westminster.

As a result, the Queen is never short of somewhere to stay when she is not abroad travelling, but there tends to be a pattern to her year.

Buckingham Palace is her usual weekday residence from Monday to Friday and effectively her 'office', where she will spend around three hours each day going through her state papers or 'doing her boxes', as she calls it. Weekends are usually spent at Windsor where she also stays for a month at Easter and for the week of Royal Ascot in June. The Queen always goes to Sandringham House immediately before Christmas and most years will stay there until early February with family coming and going. August and September mean summer holidays and the start of the shooting season, and these months are always spent at Balmoral. The Queen is also in Scotland in July for Holyrood week, when she stays at Holyrood Palace; this is her home whenever she is carrying out official duties in Scotland.

Balmoral

Of all her homes, Balmoral Castle in Aberdeenshire in Scotland holds a special place in the royal heart: 'It's nice to hibernate for a bit when one leads such a very moveable life.' She also loves the wildness of the countryside there: 'You can go out for miles and never see anybody. There are endless possibilities.'

The castle is still much as it was when she visited as a child and in fact has changed very little since Queen Victoria described it as 'My dear paradise in the Highlands'. And the Queen has said, 'There is a certain fascination in keeping the place as Queen Victoria had it.'

The famously not-amused monarch's favourite chair remains unmoved in the drawing room, although no one is allowed to sit on it. The Queen's friend and former racing manager Lord Carnavon's wife, Jean, described how the out-of-bounds chair was, ironically, something of a magnet for guests: 'Every new person goes for it, and everyone screams.'

Rumours that the Queen keeps a Billy Bass singing fish on top of a grand piano at Balmoral are unconfirmed.

Each morning while the Queen eats breakfast, a piper in full regalia marches around the castle playing the bagpipes, just as one did in Queen Victoria's day. She then attends her 'boxes' and official business but while there the Queen likes to spend as much time as possible outdoors walking her dogs and riding.

She has described Balmoral as having 'an atmosphere of its own'. And she added, 'To be able to sleep in the same bed for six weeks is a nice change.'

Princess Diana was said not to be a fan of Balmoral, and her visits there did not get off to the best start. Greeted by the Queen, closely followed by the corgis, Diana burst into tears when she realized one of the corgis was holding a mole in its mouth. An equerry commented that Her Majesty 'can't stand a blubber' and on subsequent visits by the princess she would archly suggest a mole-hunt.

Both Sally Bedell Smith and Margaret Rhodes write about the Queen's intimate knowledge of the 50,000-acre estate. Her estate manager, Martin Leslie, commented, 'Her Majesty is aware of everything.' Even the comings and goings in private lives. While driving a visitor on a tour, the Queen spotted one of her gamekeepers out with a woman. 'Hoorah!' she exclaimed, and afterwards explained that she was thrilled to see the man with a new girlfriend as he had been devastated when his wife left him.

On another occasion, on hearing that one of the chefs had proposed to a groom at Queen Victoria's favourite beauty spot, Albert's Cairn, the Queen invited them to Craigowan Lodge, where she was staying, to toast the happy couple.

Getting Stuck In

Her cousin Margaret Rhodes, who has been out deer stalking with the Queen since they were both young teenagers, says it is always fun to see the monarch out on the hills with a new stalker: 'She would be crawling on her stomach with her nose up to the soles of the stalker's boots, which would be a surprise to the stalker.'

A footman at Sandringham was extremely surprised to be asked by Her Majesty, 'Please help me. Would you pull my pants off?' The royals had returned from a morning's shooting wet and muddy. The Queen, dressed in Hunter wellingtons and Barbour waterproof leggings, was having some trouble peeling off the waterproofs.

The Queen's practical side is reflected in duties assigned to another footman – bat catching. Royal chronicler Brian Hoey recorded his story: 'In the late afternoon, it was quite common to see Her Majesty call for a butterfly net so she could catch the bats which infest the upper reaches of the castle. She would catch them in the net, hand them to me and tell me to let them go outside. She was very strict about them not being harmed. Of course, the next day, they would all come back again and we would go through the same routine. I think she enjoyed it.'

Now in her late eighties, it is to be assumed that the Queen leaves this task to someone else.

When Lucian Freud painted the Queen in 2001, his friend Clarissa Eden recounts, 'They talked about racing and horses. She kept saying, "We must stop talking. We must get on with this portrait."' One of the stories the Queen shared with him was of a rather dramatic episode at a pheasant shoot, while she was under the protection of a personal security officer. The Queen explained, 'I was picking up after the guns as I always do, when a wounded cock pheasant scratched me and drew blood. The detective assumed I'd been shot, threw himself on top of me and began giving me mouth-to-mouth resuscitation. I consider we got to know each other rather well.'

As someone who is known for her sensible attitude to life, and is hardly a daredevil, it says something about the Queen's character that she resolutely refuses to follow advice and wear a protective hard hat when out riding. Windsor Castle staff regularly joke, 'The only thing that comes between the Queen and her heir is a Hermès scarf.'

Maggie and Liz

A feature of every summer stay at Balmoral is the visit by the current prime minister and spouse, some more congenial than others. The visits by Margaret Thatcher were always interesting for observers. There was said to be a certain 'stiffness' between the two powerful women, at least in the early days. And the Queen found her first female prime minister much too deferential. She curtseyed too low and one friend admitted, 'The Queen had some most amusing and well-observed lines about Thatcher.' The Queen herself is on record saying, 'Mrs Thatcher never listens to a word I say.'

Visits followed a pattern. There would be a formal black-tie dinner on the first night, which always gave rise to some tension over Mrs Thatcher's reluctance to leave the table with the other ladies. The Prime Minister was also puzzled by the Queen's early bedtime at 11.15 p.m., which other guests were expected to observe. 'Bed? What would we do up there?' she was said to have asked on her first stay.

The traditional barbecue, always organized for the second evening by Prince Philip, was not without confusion. Mrs Thatcher was shocked that the Queen should choose to wash up afterwards herself, and – horror of horrors – with her bare hands. After one visit, Mrs Thatcher sent Her Majesty a pair of rubber gloves. On another visit, the Prime Minister was obviously very uncomfortable watching her sovereign clearing plates and kept trying to help. Finally, an irritated Queen said through gritted teeth, 'Will somebody please tell that woman to sit down?'

Like Margaret Thatcher before him, Tony Blair was said to find the informality of the Balmoral barbecues, with the Queen waiting on her guests, very odd. His wife, Cherie, however, came to 'have a soft spot for Prince Philip', with whom she shared an interest in the internet and new technology. She also liked the way the Queen played with their young son Leo, patiently teaching him how to throw biscuits to the corgis.

> Mrs Thatcher was far from a country-woman. When asked whether the premier would be joining the rest of the guests on a ramble over the hills, the Queen smiled wryly, 'I think you will find Mrs Thatcher only walks on the road.'

Margaret Thatcher may have been the 'Iron Lady', and a very strong personality, but she did not possess the Queen's physical stamina and strength. At a major reception held annually for diplomats at Buckingham Palace, when Mrs Thatcher felt faint and was forced to sit down for the second year running, the usually sympathetic Queen cast the royal eye over the PM and observed, 'Oh look! She's keeled over again.'

Quite what the Queen thought of Mrs Thatcher's infamous announcement on the birth of her son's first child, 'We are a grandmother!' is not on public record. Perhaps there is an arch comment in the private royal diary.

Although very different characters with contrasting interests, the Queen came to respect Mrs Thatcher. A former adviser said, 'As someone who inherited her position, she is interested in meritocrats.' After their regular prime ministerial Tuesday evening meetings at Buckingham Palace, Mrs Thatcher would often stay on for a whisky or two with the Queen.

Mrs Thatcher's weekly meetings with the Queen were not without their own tensions. Frequently arriving fifteen minutes early, the Prime Minister was forced to wait until the allotted time, the Queen refusing to be hurried against the agreed schedule.

A Bat Out of Hell

Although she does not hold a driving licence, the Queen learned to drive while serving with the Auxiliary Territorial Service of the Army in 1945 when she was also trained as a mechanic. At the time, her company commander pronounced her 'a very good and extremely careful and considerate driver'.

Because of her ATS training, the Queen knows how to change a wheel and a tyre.

The Queen is the only person allowed to drive without a licence, nor does she have to display registration numbers on the front and back of state vehicles, although her own personal vehicles do have number plates.

She is frequently spotted at the wheel, driving herself when staying at Balmoral and Sandringham, or one of her other country estates. These days her road skills tend to be a little more combative and assertive. Her cousin Margaret Rhodes is not the only person to have described her driving 'like a bat out of hell'. She also never wears a seat belt.

> During one such jaunt in a Land Rover around the Balmoral estate, the Queen came across a couple of men bearing shotguns and bulging sacks. Recognizing one of them as the local head of police she cheerfully remarked, 'There's nothing like catching the Chief Superintendent poaching rabbits.'

When Sir Sherard Cowper-Coles was appointed British Ambassador to Saudi Arabia in 2003, the Queen took a gleeful delight in telling him the story of how she had once terrified the late King Abdullah of Saudi Arabia.

It was during the then Crown Prince's first visit to Balmoral and after lunch he expressed an interest in seeing the estate. Land Rovers were duly brought round to the front of the castle. Prince Abdullah was more than a little surprised to find the Queen herself at the wheel as his driver and tour guide. Women in Saudi Arabia are still not allowed to drive. The Queen roared away, accelerating fast. Seemingly oblivious to her passenger's discomfort, the Queen chatted all the way, pointing out landmarks, taking her hands off the wheel and navigating the narrow estate roads at speed. Speaking through his interpreter, Prince Abdullah begged the Queen to slow down. She carried on regardless. One is Queen after all and one does so like to drive. Maybe this is one way for the normally sensible monarch to let off steam?

This is not the only account of the Queen's reckless driving. Pedestrians walking in Windsor Great Park have been terrorized by the racing royal, and there have been at least two official complaints.

Having delivered a speech on road safety in 1957, Prince Philip promptly crashed his car moments after leaving.

Kicking Back

The subject of which television programmes the royals like watching is hotly debated. They are said to enjoy soaps and have visited the different sets on several occasions. The Queen Mother's favourite was *Coronation Street*, while the rest of the family prefer *EastEnders*. When relaxing at Balmoral, box sets of *Dr Who*, detective dramas and comedies are always popular choices, and even if she doesn't watch them all, the Queen is well aware of current shows such as *The X Factor*.

> Years ago, pre-TV box recorders, a Church of England bishop preparing for evening prayer at Windsor Castle was disturbed by a knock at the door. He was surprised to find the Queen standing outside enquiring, 'Would you mind awfully putting back the time of the evening service as Mummy really wants to watch *Hi-de-Hi!*?'

Unlike Alan Bennett's fictional version of Elizabeth II in his novella *The Uncommon Reader*, who becomes obsessed by the world of books, the Queen tends not to reveal what she really likes to read. She is rumoured to enjoy detective stories and anything involving horses, making Dick Francis a favourite author and also, more surprisingly, Jilly Cooper, the racy writer of *Riders* and other country set romps.

The Queen was, however, less than impressed by T. S. Eliot, when as a child she met him and he performed a rendition of his poem 'The Wasteland'. As the Queen Mother recalled, 'We had this rather lugubrious man in a suit and he read a poem – I think it was called "The Desert". At first the girls got the giggles, then I did, then even the King.' To be fair, Eliot does not have the best reputation as a reader of his own poetry.

The Queen's cousin Margaret Rhodes, who was also Lady-in-Waiting to the Queen Mother for the last eleven years of her life, tells a story of the Queen's quick wit. One late summer evening when she and her husband, Denys, were staying at Balmoral, Princess Margaret asked Denys (a thriller writer)

how his latest book was coming along. He answered, 'It's nearly finished but I desperately need a title.' The Queen, who had just walked into the room, immediately quipped, 'And I cannot think of a reason for giving you one.'

A Royal Family Christmas

Royal Christmases follow a traditional pattern. The celebrations usually take place at Sandringham. Like her grandfather George V, who first chose the Norfolk house as the setting for the family Christmas, the Queen prefers the more homely atmosphere there. She also has many happy memories of Christmases there with her own parents.

For most people the Queen's speech is part of Christmas. Broadcast at 3 p.m. British time, not everyone watches or takes in everything she says, but we know it's there, reassuringly traditional, essential. During her Diamond Jubilee celebrations the historian Simon Schama reflected, 'There is something simple and innocent ... which people respect enormously in the Queen.' And this comes through in her Christmas messages.

In the Queen's Christmas broadcast of 1975, she said, 'It does matter what each individual does each day ... kindness, sympathy, resolution and courteous behaviour are infectious.'

Her first televised Christmas speech in 1957 stated boldly, 'I cannot lead you into battle, I do not give you laws or administer justice but I can do something else: I can give you my heart and my devotion to these old islands and to all the peoples of our brotherhood of nations.'

Buying the perfect gift for the Queen can be tricky. A shower cap from Prince Harry emblazoned with the words 'Ain't life a bitch' was reportedly a particular hit.

A white leather loo seat that Princess Anne gave her brother Charles one year also proved a surprise winner. Meant as a joke, apparently it is so comfortable he often takes it on overseas trips.

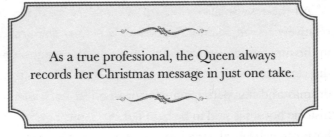

As a true professional, the Queen always records her Christmas message in just one take.

A formal dinner in the evening is followed by less formal charades and other games where the Queen can exercise her talents as an excellent mimic. This is strictly for family and close friends' eyes and ears only. Her specialities are wide ranging and her repertoire is said to include politicians like Tony Benn and Tony Blair, familiar TV characters such as René from *'Allo 'Allo!*, and a very convincing Russian President Boris Yeltsin, along with several US presidents.

She also does a perfect imitation of the Aberdeenshire accent of a Scottish church minister who, saying grace before one dinner at Balmoral, made an unfortunate choice of words: 'For the delicious meal we are about to receive, and for the intercourse afterwards, may the Lord make us truly thankful.'

Haunted Houses

A former royal adviser said, 'The Queen firmly believes in ghosts and often tells how they are present in all of her homes. She is not frightened of them, just simply fascinated.'

All the royal palaces have a long history and even the relatively recent Balmoral and Sandringham were rebuilt in the nineteenth century on the site of older estates. Over the centuries, their walls have witnessed major events and dramas and it is perhaps not surprising that each of these historic houses is said to be haunted. At Sandringham, staff have often been alarmed to see objects moving by themselves, and have shivered at inexplicable cold spots, and the Queen always wants to hear every detail. She is said to like the ghosts' presence 'because she feels they are harmless and add character to the place.' Perhaps the idea of family phantoms keeping watch is reassuring?

As children staying at Windsor Castle, Princesses Elizabeth and Margaret had their first ghostly encounter, appropriately enough glimpsing Queen Elizabeth I.

Not in Front of the Servants

Before their former nanny, Marion Crawford, spilled the beans on life with the young princesses, the Queen Mother wrote to remind her that 'people in positions of confidence with us must be utterly oyster.'

When the revelations were published in *Little Princesses* in 1950, the Queen Mother was outraged: 'We can only think that our late and completely trusted governess has gone off her head.'

Then as now, those who work closely with the royal family are in a position of trust. They are expected to abide by certain rules and never, ever speak to the press.

Members of staff can develop quite a close relationship with the royal family. They see them at all times of the day and in all sorts of circumstances. It is important that they get along. When appointing new members of staff, the Queen tactfully suggests, 'Let's try it for a couple of months to see how we get on. Then if either of us can't stand the other, we can call it a day.'

Nevertheless, stories do leak out. When there have been breaches of trust, notably when journalist Ryan Parry posed as a footman and then wrote in the newspapers about what he had seen, the Palace acted swiftly with injunctions. The Queen has remained silent on the matter, although there can be a certain frosty tightening of the lips when the subject is mentioned.

> The Queen writes with a fountain pen that belonged to her father, King George VI, and always uses black blotting paper to prevent any unscrupulous snooping into state or personal correspondence.

An excellent mimic herself, the Queen heard her own voice being impersonated by two housemaids at Sandringham. Walking the corgis in the garden she came upon the two laughing and chatting in an exaggerated version of Her Majesty. The pair were horrified when they turned to see her standing there but the Queen just smiled and carried on with her walk.

The Press

And what of the press? Journalists en masse definitely make the royal family uneasy and the royals tend to be more than a little wary of them. The royal family go out of their way to avoid certain elements of the paparazzi, and to say they watch what they say in front of the press would be an understatement.

Although he has not always been the keenest fan of newspapers, once describing the *Daily Express* as 'a bloody awful newspaper ... full of lies, scandal and imagination', after they printed a series of scandalous stories on the Palace, Prince Philip does, however, keep a collection of press cartoons of himself, which he has hung on his lavatory walls at Sandringham. One of the advantages of the estate is that the paparazzi are no longer allowed to photograph the royal family relaxing there.

The Prince's opinion of the press as something of a nuisance has not really changed over the years. As far back as 1966 he told the matron of a Caribbean hospital, 'You have mosquitoes, I have the press.'

Prince Charles has also felt provoked to shout, 'Get out of the way, you annoying little prat,' to a particularly persistent photographer. And as a more general protest, 'Down with the press!' or calling them 'Bloody people.'

Prince Harry has commented that he is not always portrayed as he really is: 'It is the media that stamp an image on me that really isn't me.'

While ceremonially planting a tree, he turned his back to photographers and joked, 'You've got the best view!'

Gin, Dubonnet and Eggs: The Full English

When it comes to food and drink, the Queen and the rest of the royal family have very definite ideas on what they do and do not like. In line with their green principles and desire to be as environmentally friendly as possible, the family do not approve of waste and can be surprisingly frugal. Princess Anne has talked about 'good old-fashioned Hanoverian housekeeping' and they can have a very practical, no-nonsense approach, but this is still royalty, with a long aristocratic lineage. They want and expect the best – just at the best price, as well.

Eating In

The Queen's wedding breakfast was served on gold plates but the main course was 'only partridge'; game was readily available whereas other meats were still strictly rationed in 1947. The full menu consisted of Filet de Sole Mountbatten, Perdreau (partridge) en Casserole and Bombe Glacée Princess Elizabeth. The nine-foot-tall, four-tiered wedding cake was made using ingredients given as gifts from abroad.

Thanks to Ryan Parry, the trainee reporter for the *Daily Mirror*, who spent several months working undercover as a footman at Buckingham Palace in the early nineties, we know quite a lot about the royal rituals.

Every morning the Queen is woken by her personal maid, who takes her a pot of Earl Grey tea and some biscuits for the dogs. At the breakfast table, cereal is kept in Tupperware containers alongside bowls of fresh fruit. Porridge oats and cornflakes are her favourite. The Queen likes her toast lightly spread with marmalade and she is an avid reader of the *Racing Post*. She is also a fan of *The Lady*, *Thoroughbred Owner and Breeder* and the *Radio Times*. Although Her Majesty no longer likes a cooked English breakfast she will sometimes opt for scrambled eggs. Prince Philip on the other hand still likes a full English and is also keen on oatcakes and honey. He drinks black coffee and, unlike his wife, rarely chooses tea.

Afternoon tea is served at five o'clock sharp and is said to be the favourite meal. Tiny crustless sandwiches, often cucumber along with an alternative, are cut into shapes resembling octagons. In a bizarre throwback to another era, rectangles or squares are said to be too coffin-like and mean the maker intends the monarch harm. There is also always cake and tea.

At the famous Balmoral barbecues guests arrive to find Prince Philip in a fog of smoke, often cursing creatively. The royal couple have a special trailer for picnics and barbecues in which everything is laid out in its proper place. The trailer attaches to one of the Land Rovers and can then be driven to the picnic site.

The Prince has devised a griddle of his own design and has a reputation as an inventive cook, trying to reproduce dishes he has been served or recipes he has watched being made on television. Ingredients tend to be prepared in advance in the castle kitchens. They are then packed into containers, labelled and sent over to the barbecue site. All the game shot on the estate is graded with the finest cuts set aside to be marinaded ready for barbecuing. The next grade tends to be used for stews and casseroles for lunches, while lesser cuts are sent to the village butcher to be made into sausages, which are also barbecued.

Afterwards, the Queen leads the clean-up and everything has to be replaced exactly as it was packed. 'Woe betide if you put the cutlery in the wrong place,' said one seasoned guest. These days the Queen usually leaves the washing-up to someone else.

Favourite Foods

According to Charles Oliver who, incredibly, worked at Buckingham Palace under Victoria, George VI and Elizabeth II, the royals all have a 'passion' for eggs. They like them fried, boiled, scrambled, poached, *en cocotte*, with mushrooms, with liver and hollandaise, in omelettes and soufflés. They are eaten at breakfast and tea, too. In line with the Queen's interest in animal welfare, she insists that all eggs used in the royal palaces are from free-range chickens and also insists 'a brown egg tastes better', no matter what science says.

Prince Charles is so fond of eggs he likes them with English muffins for afternoon tea and often asks for a poached egg to top whatever else he happens to be eating, steak and egg being a particular favourite.

The Queen loves chocolate, and chocolate biscuit cake is so popular with the family that it was even served at William and Kate's wedding. The Queen is also partial to an Australian cake known as a Lamington, where sponge squares are dipped in chocolate and then rolled in coconut. Lemon tart, coffee and chocolate mousse, and the Queen Mother's favourite After Eight ice cream are all often on the menu.

Every day the Queen writes down what she wants to eat in a menu book. This can also be used for any comments she may have on previous meals. In one she wrote, 'I found this in the salad – could you eat it?' Next to it was a small dead slug.

Eating Out

On overseas tours the Queen has been served an array of exotic and not always appetizing foods. In Belize she was served a local delicacy called a Gibnut, a large rat-like rodent similar in appearance to a chipmunk. Afterwards, she politely said it tasted like rabbit. It now regularly features in restaurants billed as 'Royal Rat'. She also gamely managed to eat a few mouthfuls of sea cucumber with chopsticks when in China. These are sea animals that resemble the vegetable but have a slippery, gel-like texture; her expression did not alter.

Both the Queen and Prince Philip are very self-disciplined and have to eat so much officially, they eat little when off-duty. The Prince in particular has hardly changed in size over the years. He was not altogether joking when he complained, 'I never see any home cooking – all I get is fancy stuff.'

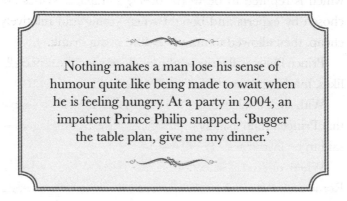

Nothing makes a man lose his sense of humour quite like being made to wait when he is feeling hungry. At a party in 2004, an impatient Prince Philip snapped, 'Bugger the table plan, give me my dinner.'

After a mammoth breakfast including eggs, bacon, smoked salmon, kedgeree, croissants and pains au chocolat prepared by French chef Régis Crépy in 2002, Prince Philip's dismissive opinion was: 'The French don't know how to cook breakfast.'

But then according to the Prince, neither can half the British population. 'British women can't cook,' he asserted, no doubt winning himself many fans among his audience at the Scottish Women's Institute in 1961.

A Tipple or Two

Since 2007 the wine cellars at Buckingham Palace have been cooled by water from a borehole in the grounds. A cold-air curtain helps to keep the temperature at an optimum 10–12 degrees Celsius, and a yeoman of the cellar, a deputy and an under butler look after the wine and spirit store kept there, which is reputed to be worth over £2 million. Wines are chosen by experts and bought when young and relatively cheap, then allowed to mature before being drunk.

Prince Philip will write on the labels of wines he especially likes, marking them 'Good' or 'Very good'.

With such a select cellar at his disposal, it seems a shame that Prince Philip usually prefers beer. Pale ale and lager are said to be favourites.

When offered a selection of the finest Italian wine in Rome on a state visit to the city in 2000, he lost all patience with Italian Prime Minister Giuliano Amato, 'I don't care what kind it is, just get me a beer!'

On being presented with a hamper of Southern foods by the US Ambassador in 1999, the Prince rifled through the contents and asked, 'Where's the Southern Comfort?'

> The royal family are all very keen on ice in their drinks but apparently detest the sound of ice cubes chinking. As a result, they have a special machine to produce round ice balls, which make a softer, less irritating noise in the glass.

Over the years there has been the occasional problem of staff drinking too much. The Queen has always been inclined to overlook the odd indiscretion by a trusted member of staff. On one occasion, coming upon a very drunk servant sprawled at the bottom of a flight of stairs, the Queen simply called for assistance, 'Would someone please come and pick Frank up, I think he's a little under the weather.'

Gin and Dubonnet was the Queen Mother's tipple of choice but never before noon. She was particular about the mix, preferring two parts Dubonnet to one part gin. When travelling she hid her supply of gin in hatboxes, reflecting, 'I couldn't get through all my royal engagements without a little something.'

Margaret Rhodes, her lady-in-waiting for the last eleven years of her life, categorically denies that the Queen Mother had a drinking habit or was over-fond of alcohol. 'Before lunch she would have a gin and Dubonnet, with a slice of lemon and a lot of ice. During the meal she might take some wine. In the evening she would have a dry Martini and a glass of champagne with her dinner.' It seems churlish to point out that this comes to at least six units of alcohol in a day, which would be classified as binge drinking according to current government guidelines.

The Queen Mother once asked a servant for a Martini and was appalled to receive a glass of the Italian vermouth rather than the gin cocktail she was expecting. As the American journalist R. W. Apple was at the same function she quizzed him: 'Young man. I believe you're American from your accent. Do you know how to make a Martini cocktail?' On hearing that indeed he did, Johnny Apple was quickly dispatched. 'Please will you go to the pantry with the butler and instruct him how to do so,' instructed the Queen Mother. The resulting drinks were very much to the Queen Mother's liking.

The Queen also enjoys gin and Dubonnet, and is partial to pink vermouth and gin Martinis, preferring them to wine. If drinking wine she tends to choose lighter hocks or even rosés but not champagne, which she actually dislikes. When proposing toasts she will take only a sip.

On one occasion, when debating whether or not to drink a second glass of wine at lunch, the Queen Mother helpfully advised, 'Don't forget, my dear, you have to reign all afternoon.'

Bibliography

Arscott, David, *Queen Elizabeth II Diamond Jubilee 60 Years a Queen: A Very Peculiar History*, Book House, 2012.

Bedell Smith, Sally, *Elizabeth the Queen*, Penguin Books, 2012.

Botham, Noel, and Bruce Montague, *The Book of Royal Useless Information*, John Blake Publishing, 2012.

Brandreth, Gyles, *Philip and Elizabeth: Portrait of a Royal Marriage*, Arrow Books, 2004.

Carey, George, *Know the Truth: A Memoir*, HarperCollins, 2004.

Crawford, Marion, *The Little Princesses*, Orion, 2003.

Crossman, Richard, *The Crossman Diaries*, ed. Anthony Howard, Hamish Hamilton, 1979.

Dampier, Phil, and Ashley Walton, *What's in the Queen's Handbag and other Royal Secrets*, Book Guild Publishing, 2007.

Hardman, Robert, *Our Queen*, Random House, 2012.

Hoey, Brian, *At Home with the Queen*, HarperCollins, 2002.

Hoey, Brian, *Not in Front of the Corgis*, The Robson Press, 2011.

Longford, Elizabeth, *Elizabeth R*, Weidenfeld & Nicolson, 1983.

Marr, Andrew, *The Diamond Queen: Elizabeth II and Her People*, Macmillan UK, 2011.

Parker, Michael, *It's All Going Terribly Wrong*, Bene Factum Publishing, 2013.

Petrella, Kate, *Royal Wisdom: The Most Daft, Cheeky, and Brilliant Quotes from Britain's Royal Family*, Adams Media, 2011.

Rhodes, Margaret, *The Final Curtsey*, Birlinn Ltd and Umbria Press, 2012.

Websites:

www.allgreatquotes.com

www.bbc.co.uk

www.biography.com

www.brainyquote.com

www.britroyals.com

www.dailymail.co.uk

www.express.co.uk

www.facebook.com/TheBritishMonarchy

www.famousquotesandauthors.com

www.guardian.co.uk

www.hellomagazine.com

www.huffingtonpost.com

www.independent.co.uk

www.mirror.co.uk

news.sky.com

uk.reuters.com

www.royal.gov.uk

www.saidwhat.com

www.thinkexist.com

www.time.com

www.thetimes.co.uk

www.vanityfair.com

www.vox.com

en.wikipedia.org

Elizabeth R